enVisionmath 2.0

Volume 2B Topics 13-15

Authors

Randall I. Charles
Professor Emeritus
Department of Mathematics
San Jose State University
San Jose, California

Jennifer Bay-Williams
Professor of Mathematics Education
College of Education and Human
Development
University of Louisville
Louisville, Kentucky

Robert Q. Berry, III
Associate Professor of
Mathematics Education
Department of Curriculum,
Instruction and Special Education
University of Virginia
Charlottesville, Virginia

Janet H. Caldwell
Professor of Mathematics
Rowan University
Glassboro, New Jersey

Zachary Champagne
Assistant in Research
Florida Center for Research in Science,
Technology, Engineering, and
Mathematics (FCR-STEM)
Jacksonville, Florida

Juanita Copley
Professor Emerita, College of Education
University of Houston
Houston, Texas

Warren Crown
Professor Emeritus of Mathematics
Education
Graduate School of Education
Rutgers University
New Brunswick, New Jersey

Francis (Skip) Fennell
L. Stanley Bowlsbey Professor
of Education and Graduate and
Professional Studies
McDaniel College
Westminster, Maryland

Karen Karp
Professor of Mathematics Education
Department of Early Childhood and
Elementary Education
University of Louisville
Louisville, Kentucky

Stuart J. Murphy
Visual Learning Specialist
Boston, Massachusetts

Jane F. Schielack
Professor of Mathematics
Associate Dean for Assessment and
Pre K-12 Education, College of Science
Texas A&M University
College Station, Texas

Jennifer M. Suh
Associate Professor for
Mathematics Education
George Mason University
Fairfax, Virginia

Jonathan A. Wray
Mathematics Instructional Facilitator
Howard County Public Schools
Ellicott City, Maryland

SAVVAS
LEARNING COMPANY

MW01105930

Mathematicians

Roger Howe
Professor of Mathematics
Yale University
New Haven, Connecticut

Gary Lippman
Professor of Mathematics and
Computer Science
California State University, East Bay
Hayward, California

ELL Consultants

Janice R. Corona
Independent Education Consultant
Dallas, Texas

Jim Cummins
Professor
The University of Toronto
Toronto, Canada

Debbie Crisco
Math Coach
Beebe Public Schools
Beebe, Arkansas

Kathleen A. Cuff
Teacher
Kings Park Central School District
Kings Park, New York

Erika Doyle
Math and Science Coordinator
Richland School District
Richland, Washington

Reviewers

Susan Jarvis
Math and Science Curriculum Coordinator
Ocean Springs Schools
Ocean Springs, Mississippi

ISBN-13: 978-0-328-93069-2
ISBN-10: 0-328-93069-5
5 20

TOPIC 13 More Addition, Subtraction, and Length

Essential Question: How can you add and subtract lengths?

Look at the big waves! Look at the big rock!

Water and land in an area can have different sizes and shapes.

Wow! Let's do this project and learn more.

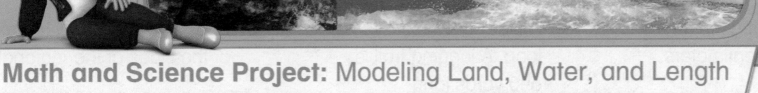

Math and Science Project: Modeling Land, Water, and Length

Find Out Find and share books and other sources that show the shapes and kinds of land and water in an area. Draw a picture or make a model to show the land or water in an area.

Journal: Make a Book Show what you learn in a book. In your book, also:

- Draw a picture to show the shape of some land or water in your area.

- Make up a math story about lengths. Draw a picture to show how to solve the problem in your story.

Name _____

Review What You Know

1. Circle the measuring unit that is better to **estimate** the **length** of a room.

   meter

   centimeter

2. Circle the number of feet in 1 **yard**.

   2 feet

   3 feet

   4 feet

   12 feet

3. The clock shows the time a math class begins. Circle **a.m.** or **p.m.**

   a.m.

   p.m.

Estimate

4. **Estimate** the length of the eraser in centimeters.

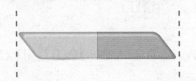

   About _____ centimeters

Compare

5. A sidewalk is 632 yards long. A jogging trail is 640 yards long.

   Use <, >, or = to compare the lengths.

   632 ◯ 640

Rectangles

6. Label the 2 missing lengths of the sides of the rectangle.

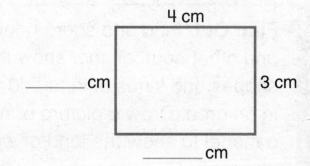

4 cm

_____ cm

3 cm

_____ cm

Name _____

Solve & Share

What is the total distance around the blue rectangle in centimeters? Show your work. Did you add or subtract?

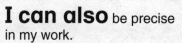

I can ...
solve problems by adding or subtracting length measurements.

I can also be precise in my work.

___ ◯ ___ ◯ ___ ◯ ___ = ___

The distance around the blue rectangle is _____ centimeters.

The book is 9 inches long and 6 inches wide.

What is the distance around the front cover of the book?

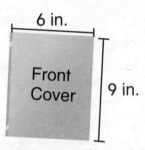

6 in.

Front Cover

9 in.

Add the lengths of all four sides to find the distance around the cover.

$9 + 6 + 9 + 6 = ?$

$18 + 12 =$

$10 + 10 + 8 + 2 =$

$20 + 10 = 30$

The distance around the cover is 30 inches.

How much longer is the teacher's arm than the child's arm?

Think: Will I add or subtract?

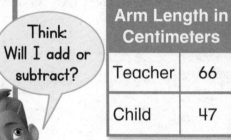

Arm Length in Centimeters	
Teacher	66
Child	47

Subtract to compare measurements.

$66 - 47 = ?$

$$\begin{array}{r} 5\,\,6 \\ \cancel{6}\,\cancel{6} \\ -\,4\,7 \\ \hline 19 \end{array}$$

The teacher's arm is 19 centimeters longer than the child's arm.

Do You Understand?

Show Me! Explain how to find the distance around a square park that is 2 miles long on each side.

☆ **Guided Practice** ☆ Decide if you need to add or subtract. Then write an equation to help solve each problem.

1. What is the distance around the baseball card?

$10 + 7 + 10 + 7 = 34$

Distance around: __34__ cm

10 cm

7 cm

2. What is the distance around the puzzle?

Distance around: _____ in.

15 in.

12 in.

Topic 13 | Lesson 1

Name _____

Independent Practice

Decide if you need to add or subtract.
Then write an equation to help solve each problem.

3. What is the distance around the door?

3 ft

7 ft

_____

Distance around: _____ ft

---

4. What is the distance around the cell phone?

2 in.

4 in.

_____

Distance around: _____ in.

---

5. How much longer is the red scarf than the blue scarf?

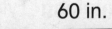

60 in.

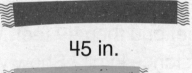

45 in.

_____

_____ in. longer

---

6. Algebra What is the length of the shorter side of the rectangle? Complete the equation to solve.

20 cm

?

$20 + \underline{\quad} + 20 + \underline{\quad} = 60$

The shorter side is _____ centimeters.

Decide if you need to add or subtract.
Then write an equation to help solve each problem.

An equation is a model.

7. **Model** Ashley's sunflower is 70 inches tall. Kwame's sunflower is 60 inches tall. How much taller is Ashley's sunflower than Kwame's sunflower?

70 in.   60 in.

_____   _____ inches taller

8. **Model** Ben measures the length of a leaf and a plant. The leaf is 15 centimeters. The plant is 37 centimeters. How much shorter is the leaf than the plant?

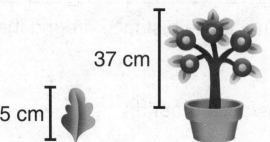

37 cm

15 cm

_____   _____ centimeters shorter

9. **Higher Order Thinking** Tyler threw a ball 42 feet and then 44 feet. Sanjay threw a ball 38 feet and then 49 feet. Who threw the longer distance in all? Show your work.

10. ✓**Assessment** What is the distance around the placemat?

Ⓐ 28 in.

Ⓑ 39 in.   11 in.

Ⓒ 56 in.

Ⓓ 66 in.

17 in.

Name _____

Another Look!

You can use addition or subtraction to solve problems with measurements. How much longer is the snake than the worm?

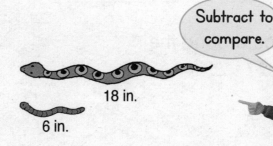
18 in.

6 in.

Subtract to compare.

$18 - 6 = 12$

The snake is __12 inches__ longer than the worm.

HOME ACTIVITY Ask your child to find a rectangular object (*a book, piece of paper, tile, etc.*). Have your child measure each side in inches and write an equation to find the distance around the object.

Decide if you need to add or subtract.
Then write an equation to help solve each problem.

1. How much shorter is the feather than the ribbon?

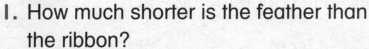
7 cm

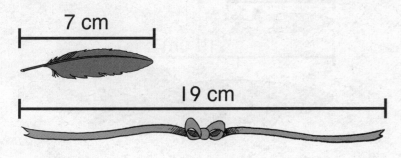
19 cm

_____

_____ centimeters shorter

2. What is the distance around the rug?

28 in.

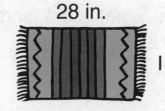
15 in.

_____

_____ inches

Decide if you need to add or subtract.
Then write an equation to help solve each problem.

3. **Model** What is the distance around the
front cover of the game box?

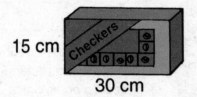

15 cm
30 cm

_____

The distance around the game

box is _____.

You can model a
problem with an equation.
Include the units in
your answer.

4. **Higher Order Thinking** The distance
around Tim's rectangular book is
48 centimeters. The length of each longer
side is 14 cm. What is the length of each
shorter side? Show your work.

_____

_____

Each shorter side of the book is

_____ long.

5. ✓**Assessment** How much longer is the
green fish than the blue fish?

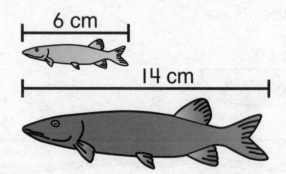

6 cm

14 cm

Ⓐ 7 cm   Ⓒ 20 cm

Ⓑ 8 cm   Ⓓ 40 cm

Name _____

Solve & Share

Julie and Steve each cut a piece of yarn.
The total length of both pieces is 12 cm.

Use centimeter cubes to measure each piece of yarn.
Circle Julie and Steve's pieces. Then explain your thinking.

I can ...
add or subtract to solve
problems about measurements.

I can also make math
arguments.

_____
_____
_____

Michelle jumped 24 inches. Tim jumped 7 fewer inches than Michelle. How far did Tim jump?

What operation should I use?

You can write a subtraction equation to show the problem.

The length of Tim's jump is unknown.

$$24 - 7 = ?$$

length of Michelle's jump · fewer inches · length of Tim's jump

You can draw a picture, such as a yardstick. Then count back to solve the problem.

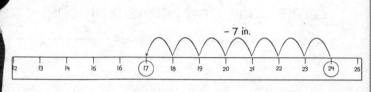

Tim jumped 17 inches.

Do You Understand?

Show Me! How does drawing a yardstick help you solve the problem above?

☆ **Guided Practice** ☆ Write an equation using a ? for the unknown number. Solve with a picture or another way.

1. A stamp measures 2 centimeters in length. How many centimeters long are two stamps?

$$2 + 2 = ?$$

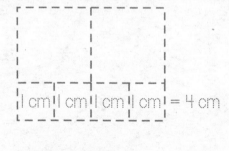

1 cm 1 cm 1 cm 1 cm = 4 cm

_____ cm

2. Stuart's desk is 64 centimeters long. His dresser is 7 centimeters longer than his desk. How long is Stuart's dresser?

_____ cm

Topic 13 | Lesson 2

Tools   Assessment

Independent Practice

Write an equation using a ? for the unknown number.
Solve with a picture or another way.

3. Filipe's pencil box is 24 centimeters long.
   Joe's pencil box is 3 centimeters shorter
   than Filipe's. How long is Joe's pencil box?

   _____   _____ cm

4. Clark threw a red ball and a blue ball. He
   threw the red ball 17 feet. He threw the
   blue ball 7 feet farther. How far did Clark
   throw the blue ball?

   _____   _____ ft

5. **Math and Science** Ashlie's map shows
   where animals, land, and water are at
   a zoo.

   The distance around her map is 38 inches.
   What is the length of the missing side?

   _____

   _____ inches

8 in.

11 in.   ? in.

8 in.

Problem Solving ⭐ Solve each problem.

6. Make Sense A brown puppy is 43 centimeters tall. A spotted puppy is 7 centimeters shorter than the brown puppy. A white puppy is 14 centimeters taller than the brown puppy. How tall is the spotted puppy? Think about what you need to find.

_____ cm

7. A-Z Vocabulary Complete the sentences using the terms below.

foot   yard   inch

A paper clip is about 1 _____ long.

My math book is about 1 _____ long.

A baseball bat is about 1 _____ long.

8. Higher Order Thinking Jack jumped 15 inches. Tyler jumped 1 inch less than Jack and 2 inches more than Randy. Who jumped the farthest? How far did each person jump?

9. ✓Assessment Kim was 48 inches tall in January. She grew 9 inches during the year. How tall is Kim at the end of the year? Write an equation with an unknown and then draw a picture to solve.

_____

_____ in.

Name _____

Homework & Practice 13-2
Find Unknown Measurements

Another Look!

Lance's boat is 13 meters long.
Cory's boat is 7 meters longer.
How long is Cory's boat?

You can follow these steps to solve word problems.

Step 1 Write an equation to show the problem. $13 + 7 = ?$

Step 2 Draw a picture to help solve.

Step 3 Solve the problem. Cory's boat is 20 meters long.

You can draw a picture to help.

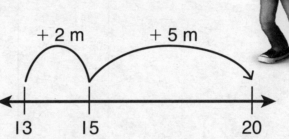
+ 2 m   + 5 m
13   15   20

HOME ACTIVITY Have your child draw a picture to solve this problem. *A building is 24 meters tall. The tree next to the building is 5 meters tall. How much shorter is the tree than the building?*

Write an equation using a ? for the unknown number. Solve with a picture or another way.

1. Suzy's ribbon is 83 centimeters long.
She cuts off 15 centimeters. How long is
Suzy's ribbon now?

_____   _____ cm

Solve each problem.

2. Jackie's shoelaces are 13 inches, 29 inches, and 58 inches long. What is the total length of all of Jackie's shoelaces? Draw a picture and write an equation to solve.

_____ in.

3. **Reasoning** Mary is 2 inches taller than Bill. Bill is 48 inches tall. How tall is Mary?

4. **Higher Order Thinking** Kyle's bedroom is 11 feet long. Garrett's bedroom is 2 feet longer than Kyle's room. Priya's bedroom is 3 feet shorter than Garrett's room. What is the sum of the lengths of Garrett and Priya's bedrooms?

_____ ft

5. ✅**Assessment** Ryan's desk is 25 inches tall. His floor lamp is 54 inches tall. How many inches taller is Ryan's floor lamp? Write an equation and draw a picture to solve.

_____ inches taller

Name _____

Solve & Share

Alex has a piece of ribbon that is 45 feet long.
He cuts the ribbon. Now he has 39 feet of ribbon.
How many feet of ribbon did Alex cut off?

Draw a picture and write an equation to solve.
Show your work.

I can ...
add and subtract to solve
measurement problems by
using drawings and equations.

I can also model
with math.

_____ ⃝ _____ = _____

A string is 28 cm. Alex cuts off a piece. Now the string is 16 cm. How long is the piece of string Alex cut off?

You can write an addition or subtraction equation.

$$28 \quad - \quad ? \quad = \quad 16$$

length at first   length cut   length now

$$16 \quad + \quad ? \quad = \quad 28$$

length now   length cut   length at first

You can draw a picture for $28 - ? = 16$ or $16 + ? = 28$.

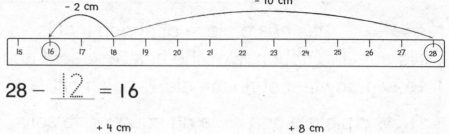

$$28 - \underline{12} = 16$$

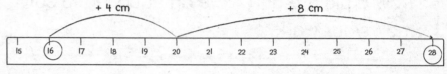

$$16 + \underline{12} = 28$$

Alex cut off 12 cm of string.

Do You Understand?

Show Me! How does writing an equation help you solve the problem above?

☆ Guided Practice ☆

Write an equation using a ? for the unknown number. Solve with a picture or another way.

1. A plant was 15 inches tall. It grew and is now 22 inches tall. How many inches did the plant grow?

+ 5 in.   + 2 in.

14 15 16 17 18 19 20 21 22 23

$$15 + ? = 22$$

2. Each bus is 10 meters long. Each boat is 7 meters long. What is the total length of two buses and two boats?

Name _____

Tools Assessment

Write an equation using a ? for the unknown number.
Solve with a picture or another way.

3. Brent's rope is 49 inches long. He cuts off
   some of the rope and now it is 37 inches long.
   How much rope did Brent cut off?

   _____   _____

4. Sue ran for some meters and stopped. Then
   she ran another 22 meters for a total of
   61 meters in all. How many meters did she run
   at first?

   _____   _____

5. **Algebra** Solve each equation. Use the chart.

○	=	12
☆	=	39
△	=	42
□	=	57

○ + ☆ = _____

□ − ☆ = _____

☆ + △ + ○ = _____

6. Make Sense The yellow boat is 15 feet shorter than the green boat. The green boat is 53 feet long. How long is the yellow boat? Think about what you are trying to find.

Write an equation to solve. Show your work.

_____ ft

7. A-Z Vocabulary Steve measured the length of his desk. It measured 2 units.

Circle the unit Steve used.

meter　　**foot**　　**centimeter**　　**inch**

Lori measured the length of her cat. It measured 45 units.

Circle the unit Lori used.

centimeter　　**yard**　　**inch**　　**foot**

8. Higher Order Thinking Lucy's ribbon is 1 foot long. Kathleen's ribbon is 15 inches long. Whose ribbon is longer and by how many inches? Explain your thinking.

_____

_____

_____

_____

9. ✓Assessment Mary's water bottle is 25 cm long. Joey's water bottle is 22 cm long. Ella's water bottle is 17 cm long.

Which statements are correct? Choose all that apply.

☐ Mary's bottle is 8 cm longer than Ella's.

☐ Joey's bottle is 6 cm longer than Ella's.

☐ Joey's bottle is 3 cm shorter than Mary's.

☐ Ella's bottle is 8 cm longer than Mary's.

Name _____

Another Look!

Kelsey is 59 inches tall.
She grows and is now 73 inches tall.
How many inches did Kelsey grow?

Show the problem with an equation: $59 + ? = 73$.

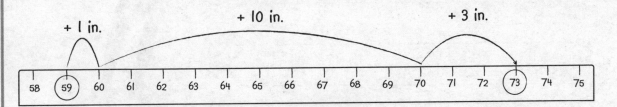

Kelsey grew 14 inches.

You can draw a picture of a tape measure to solve the problem.

HOME ACTIVITY Have your child draw a picture and write an equation to solve this problem. *Paul has 45 feet of string. Sal cuts some string off. Now Paul has 38 feet of string. How many feet of string did Sal cut off?*

Write an equation using a ? for the unknown number. Solve with a picture or another way.

1. Brigit has a piece of rope. She ties 18 more meters of rope to her rope. Now the rope is 27 meters long. How long was the rope to begin with?

Solve each problem.

Remember to use the correct words and symbols to explain your thinking.

2. **Explain** Elizabeth ran 36 meters.
Haruki ran 8 fewer meters than Elizabeth.
Delilah ran 3 fewer meters than Haruki.
How many meters did Delilah run?
Explain your thinking.

_____

_____

_____

3. **Higher Order Thinking** The lengths of the pencils are given at the right.

Write and solve a two-step problem about the pencils.

_____

_____

_____

_____

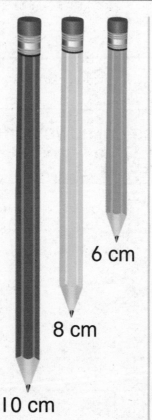

6 cm

8 cm

10 cm

4. ✓**Assessment** A hammer is 1 foot long. A car is 15 feet long. A shovel is 4 feet long.

Which statements are correct? Choose all that apply.

☐ The car is 9 ft longer than the hammer.

☐ The hammer is 14 ft shorter than the car.

☐ The shovel is 3 ft longer than the hammer.

☐ The car is 11 feet longer than the shovel.

Name _____

Solve & Share

Amelia walks 18 blocks on Monday and 5 blocks on Tuesday. How many blocks does she walk in all?

Use the number line to show how many blocks Amelia walks. Then write an equation to show your work.

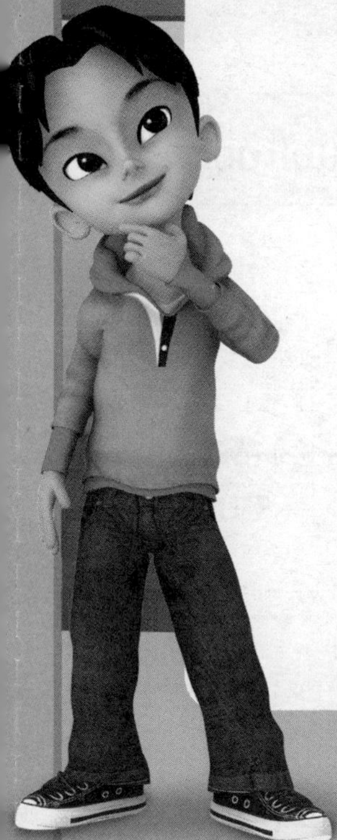

I can ...
add and subtract on a number line.

I can also model with math.

0   5   10   15   20   25   30

_____ ◯ _____ = _____

Amelia walks 17 blocks before dinner. She walks 8 blocks after dinner. How many blocks does she walk in all?

You can use a number line to add lengths.
First, show the 17 blocks Amelia walks before dinner.
Then, add the 8 blocks she walks after dinner.

Start at 0.

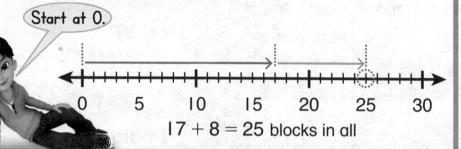

$17 + 8 = 25$ blocks in all

Amelia buys 17 feet of rope. She cuts off 8 feet of rope to make a jump rope. How many feet of rope does she have left?

You can also use a number line to subtract lengths.
First, show the 17 feet of rope.
Then, subtract the 8 feet of rope she cuts off.

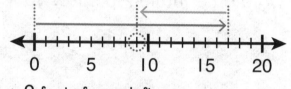

$17 - 8 = 9$ feet of rope left

Do You Understand?

Show Me! Explain how to add 14 inches and 11 inches using a number line.

☆ Guided Practice   Use the number lines to add or subtract.

1. $21 + 7 = \underline{28}$

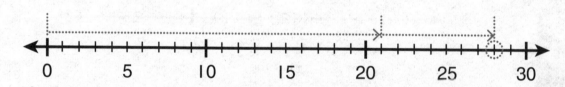

2. $28 - 14 = \underline{}$

Topic 13 | Lesson 4

Independent Practice ☆ Use the number lines to add or subtract.

3. $80 - 35 = $ _____

4. $19 + 63 = $ _____

5. Higher Order Thinking Use the number line to show 15 inches plus 0 inches. Explain your thinking.

_____

6. Number Sense Show each number below as a length from 0 on the number line. Draw four separate arrows.

9   14   24   28

Problem Solving   Use the number line to solve each problem.

7. Use Tools A football team gains 15 yards on its first play. The team gains 12 yards on its second play. How many yards does the team gain in two plays?

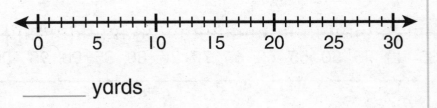

_____ yards

8. Use Tools Mia buys 25 feet of board. She uses 16 feet of board for a sandbox. How many feet of board does she have left?

A number line is a tool you can use to add and subtract.

_____ feet

9. Higher Order Thinking The runners on the track team ran 12 miles on Monday. On Tuesday, they ran 6 more miles than they ran on Monday. How many miles did they run in all on both days?

_____ miles

10. ✅ **Assessment** Deb has two pencils. One pencil is 9 cm long and the other pencil is 13 cm long. What is the total length of both pencils?

Use the number line to show your work.

_____ centimeters

782 seven hundred eighty-two

Name _____

Another Look!

$10 + 19 = ?$

Start at 0. Draw an arrow to show the first length.

Then draw a second arrow that points right to add or left to subtract.

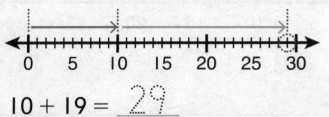

$10 + 19 = \underline{29}$

$19 - 13 = ?$

You can add or subtract on a number line.

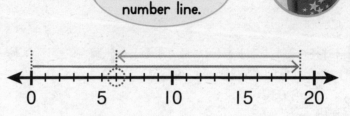

$19 - 13 = \underline{6}$

HOME ACTIVITY Measure the length of a fork and a spoon in centimeters. Then draw a number line to show how you would find the total length of the two objects.

Use the number lines to add or subtract.

1. $31 - 24 = \underline{}$

2. $18 + 23 = \underline{}$

3. **Number Sense** Look at the number line. Write the equation that it shows.

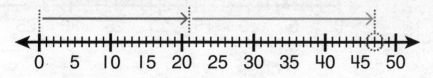

_____ ◯ _____ = _____

4. One box has 15 centimeters of ribbon. Another box has 14 centimeters of ribbon. How many centimeters of ribbon are in both boxes?

_____ centimeters

5. Susan kicks a ball 26 yards to Joe. Then, Joe kicks the ball 18 yards straight back to Susan. How far is the ball from Susan now?

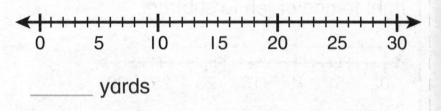

_____ yards

6. **Higher Order Thinking** Henry is painting a 38 foot fence. He paints 17 feet in the morning. He paints 16 more feet after lunch. How many feet of fence are still left to paint?

You can draw a number line to help.

_____ feet

7. ✔**Assessment** Sam has 38 inches of yarn. He gives 23 inches of yarn to Lars. How many inches of yarn does Sam have now? Show your work on the number line.

_____ inches

Name _____

Solve & Share

Choose a tool to solve each part of the problem. Be ready to explain which tools you used and why.

Which line is longer? How much longer?
Draw a line that is that length.

I can ...
choose the best tool to use to solve problems.

I can also measure and compare lengths.

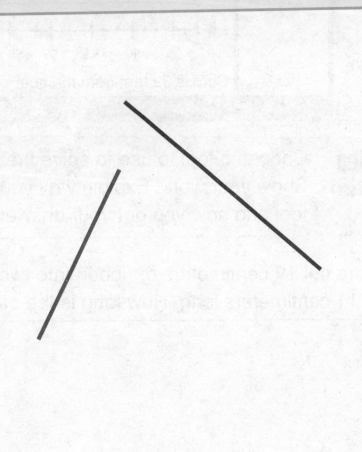

Thinking Habits

Which of these tools can I use?

counters   paper and pencil
cubes   place-value blocks
measuring tools   technology
number line

Am I using the tool correctly?

Sara plays soccer. She is 56 feet away from the goal. Then she runs 24 feet straight towards the goal.

How many feet from the goal is Sara now?

How can I use a tool to help me solve the problem?

I can think of tools that could help me. Then I can choose the best tool to use.

Tools

counters	paper and pencil
cubes	place-value blocks
measuring tools	technology
number line	

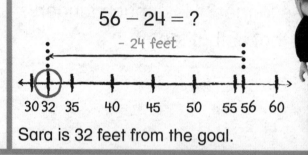

I don't need a measuring tool. The units are given in feet. I need to subtract. I will draw a number line.

$$56 - 24 = ?$$

Sara is 32 feet from the goal.

I can use paper and pencil to check my work.

$$\begin{array}{r} 56 \\ -\ 24 \\ \hline 32 \end{array}$$

Do You Understand?

Show Me! Explain why counters are **NOT** the best tool to use to solve the problem above.

☆ **Guided Practice** ☆ Choose a tool to use to solve the problem. Show your work. Explain why you chose that tool and how you got your answer.

1. Sara cut 19 centimeters of ribbon into two pieces. One piece is 11 centimeters long. How long is the other piece?

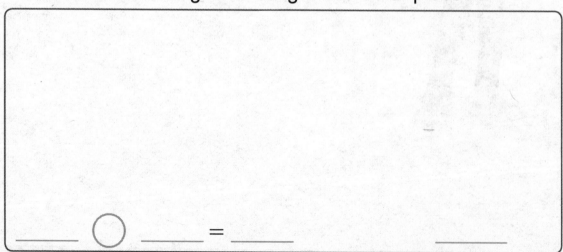

____ ◯ ____ = ____

Tools Assessment

Independent Practice ☆ Solve each problem. Show your work.

2. Work with a partner. Measure each other's arm from the shoulder to the tip of the index finger. Measure to the nearest inch. Whose arm is longer and by how much?

Choose a tool to use to solve the problem. Explain why you chose that tool and how you got your answer.

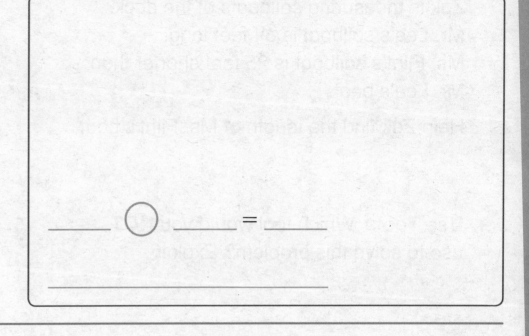

_____ ◯ _____ = _____

_____

3. Marcel jumped 39 centimeters high. Jamal jumped 48 centimeters high. How much higher did Jamal jump than Marcel?

Which tool would you **NOT** use to solve this problem? Explain.

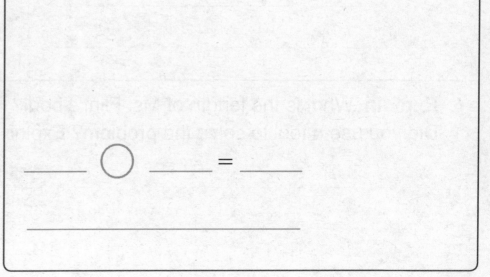

_____ ◯ _____ = _____

_____

Problem Solving

Sailboats

Zak is measuring sailboats at the dock.
Mr. Lee's sailboat is 64 feet long.
Ms. Flint's sailboat is 25 feet shorter than
Mr. Lee's boat.

Help Zak find the length of Ms. Flint's boat.

4. **Use Tools** Which tool would you **NOT**
use to solve this problem? Explain.

_____

_____

_____

5. **Be Precise** Will you add or subtract to
solve the problem? _____

Write an equation. Use ? for the unknown.

What unit of measure will you use?

_____

6. **Explain** What is the length of Ms. Flint's boat?
Did you use a tool to solve the problem? Explain.

_____

_____

_____

Another Look! What tool would you use to solve this problem?

Valerie drives 21 miles on Monday and 49 miles on Tuesday.
How many miles does she drive in all?

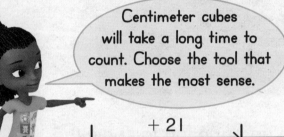

Centimeter cubes will take a long time to count. Choose the tool that makes the most sense.

You can draw a number line to solve this problem.

HOME ACTIVITY Ask your child to explain what tool he or she would use to solve this problem: *Measure the length of a door and a window to the nearest foot. How much longer is the door than the window?*

+ 21   + 49

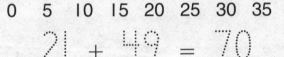

0   5   10   15   20   25   30   35   40   45   50   55   60   65   70

21 + 49 = 70

Valerie drives 70 miles in all.

Choose a tool to help you solve the problem. Show your work.
Explain why you chose that tool and how you got your answer.

1. Aaron was 38 inches tall when he was 4 years old. Aaron is 8 years old and 47 inches tall. How many inches did Aaron grow?

Trains

Mr. Bolt needs to measure the length of a train.
The first car is the engine car. It is 8 meters long.
There are also four boxcars. Each boxcar is
12 meters long.

Help Mr. Bolt find the total length of the train.

2. **Make Sense** What information is given?
   What do you need to find?

   _____

   _____

   _____

   _____

3. **Model** Write an equation to show the
   unknown.

   _____

   What unit of measure will you use?

   _____

4. **Use Tools** What is the total length of the train?
   Choose a tool to solve the problem. Show your work. _____

Follow the Path

Color a path from **Start** to **Finish**. Follow the sums and differences that are odd numbers. You can only move up, down, right, or left.

TOPIC 13 **Fluency Practice Activity**

I can ...
add and subtract within 100.

Start								
80 − 23	94 − 73	21 + 22	45 + 36	19 + 24	86 − 53	14 + 15	25 − 17	35 + 49
65 − 21	97 − 35	35 + 23	12 + 20	98 − 12	74 − 48	27 + 48	54 + 46	53 − 31
51 + 21	35 + 52	28 + 43	18 + 31	51 − 38	79 − 24	95 − 30	61 − 29	30 + 24
55 − 27	60 − 17	27 + 39	29 + 49	62 − 28	36 + 56	59 − 31	42 − 26	87 − 45
36 + 16	38 + 25	88 − 53	33 + 18	34 + 49	45 − 32	62 − 23	97 − 38	19 + 74

Finish

Vocabulary Review

Glossary

Word List
- centimeter (cm)
- foot (ft)
- height
- inch (in.)
- length
- mental math
- meter (m)
- yard (yd)

Understand Vocabulary

Choose a term from the Word List to complete each sentence.

1. The length of your finger can best be measured in centimeters or _____.

2. 100 _____ equals 1 meter.

3. _____ is how tall an object is from bottom to top.

Write T for *true* or F for *false*.

4. _____ 1 yard is 5 feet long.

5. _____ 12 inches is 1 foot long.

6. _____ A centimeter is longer than a meter.

7. _____ You can do mental math in your head.

Use Vocabulary in Writing

8. Tell how to find the total length of two pieces of string. One piece of string is 12 inches long. The other piece is 9 inches long. Use terms from the Word List.

_____
_____
_____
_____

Name _____

Set A

What is the distance around the front of the bookcase?

4 ft

3 ft

Add the lengths. Write an equation.

$4 + 3 + 4 + 3 =$ ___14___

Distance around: ___14___ feet

Write an equation to help solve.

1. What is the distance around the front of the crayon box?

12 cm

9 cm

Opposite sides have equal measures.

_____

Distance around: _____ cm

Set B

A kite string is 27 feet long.
Some of the string is cut off.
Now the kite string is 18 feet long.
How many feet of kite string were cut off?

Write an equation and draw a picture.

$27 - ? = 18$ or $18 + ? = 27$

- 9 ft

| 15 | 16 | 17 | 18 | 19 | 20 | 21 | 22 | 23 | 24 | 25 | 26 | 27 | 28 | 29 | 30 |

_27_ − _9_ = _18_   _9_ feet

Write an equation using a symbol, ?, for the unknown number. Then draw a picture to solve.

2. A piece of yarn is 42 inches long. Mia cuts some of it off. It is now 26 inches long. How much yarn did Mia cut off?

_____

A book measures 10 inches long. Another book measures 13 inches long. What is the total length of both books?

You can show 10 + 13 on a number line.

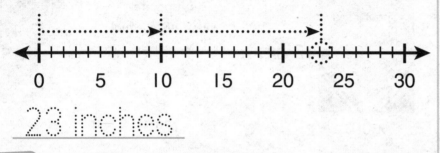

0   5   10   15   20   25   30

23 inches

Thinking Habits

Use Tools

Which of these tools can I use?

counters   paper and pencil
cubes   place-value blocks
measuring tools   technology
number line

Am I using the tool correctly?

Solve the problem using the number line.

3. One room in Jackie's house is 15 feet long. Another room is 9 feet long. What is the total length of both rooms?

0   5   10   15   20   25   30

Choose a tool to solve the problem.

4. Damon's shoelace is 45 inches long. His shoelace breaks. One piece is 28 inches long. How long is the other piece?

Explain your solution and why you chose the tool you used.

_____ ◯ _____ = _____ _____

Name _____

1. What is the distance around the cover of the notepad?

7 in.

5 in.

Distance around: _____ in.

2. Kate is 48 inches tall. Tom is 2 inches taller than Kate. James is 3 inches shorter than Tom.

How tall is James?

Ⓐ 45 inches   Ⓒ 50 inches

Ⓑ 47 inches   Ⓓ 53 inches

3. Alexis has a rope that is 7 feet long. Mariah's rope is 9 feet long. Sam's rope is 3 feet longer than Mariah's rope.

Use the measurements on the cards to complete each sentence.

| 2 feet | 5 feet | 12 feet |

Sam's rope is _____ long.

Alexis's rope is _____ shorter than Mariah's rope.

Sam's rope is _____ longer than Alexis's rope.

4. Joe rides his bike 18 miles. Then he rides 7 more miles.

Use the number line to find how far Joe rides. Then explain your work.

0   5   10   15   20   25   30

5. Pat says that each unknown equals 25 cm. Do you agree? Choose Yes or No.

47 cm + ? = 72 cm   ◯ Yes   ◯ No

? + 39 cm = 54 cm   ◯ Yes   ◯ No

99 cm − 64 cm = ?   ◯ Yes   ◯ No

93 cm − ? = 68 cm   ◯ Yes   ◯ No

6. Grace got a plant that was 34 cm tall. The plant grew and now it is 42 cm tall. How many centimeters did the plant grow?

Ⓐ   8 cm   Ⓒ   42 cm

Ⓑ   12 cm   Ⓓ   76 cm

7. Claire rides her bike 26 miles on Saturday and Sunday. She rides 8 miles on Sunday. How many miles does she ride on Saturday?

Write an equation to show the unknown.
Then use the number line to solve the problem.

_____ ◯ _____ = _____

_____ miles

8. Chris had a string that is 18 cm long. He cut off 7 cm. How much string is left?

Part A Which of these tools could you use to solve the problem? Choose all that apply.

☐   centimeter ruler

☐   paper and pencil

☐   number line

☐   inch ruler

Part B Write an equation to show the unknown. Then draw a number line to solve.

_____ ◯ _____ = _____

_____ cm

    Topic 13 | Assessment

Name _____

Fishing Fun

Jim and his family go on a fishing trip. They use a boat and fishing gear to help them catch fish.

1. Jim takes this fishing box with him. What is the distance around the front of the fishing box? Write an equation to help solve the problem.

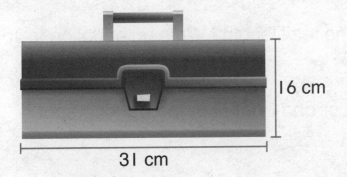

16 cm

31 cm

Distance around: _____ centimeters

2. Jim's fishing pole is 38 inches long. His dad's fishing pole is 96 inches long. How much shorter is Jim's pole than his dad's pole?

Part A Write a subtraction equation that shows the problem.

_____

Part B Solve the problem.

_____ inches shorter

3. Jim catches a fish 49 yards away from the shore. Later, he helps row the boat closer to the shore. Now he is 27 yards away from the shore. How many yards closer to shore is Jim now than when he caught the fish?

Part A Write an addition equation that shows the problem.

_____

Part B Solve the problem.

_____ yards

4. Jim catches a silver fish that is 12 inches long. His sister catches a green fish that is 27 inches long.

What is the total length of both fish? Use the number line to solve.

_____ inches

5. Jim has 27 yards of fishing line. He gives 12 yards of line to a friend. How many yards of line does Jim have left?

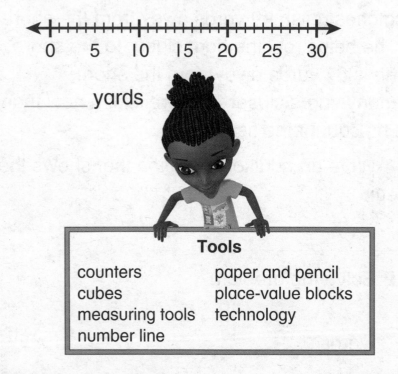

_____ yards

Tools

counters   paper and pencil
cubes   place-value blocks
measuring tools   technology
number line

6. Jim's family meets a man with a big boat. A parking spot at the dock is 32 feet long. Will the man's car and boat fit in the parking spot?

7 feet   2 feet   21 feet

Part A

What do you need to find? _____

_____

_____

Part B

What is the total length? Write an equation to solve.

_____   _____

Will the car and boat fit in the parking spot? Explain.

_____

_____

What tool did you use? _____

 Topic 13 | Performance Assessment

TOPIC 14 Graphs and Data

Essential Question: How can line plots, bar graphs, and picture graphs be used to show data and answer questions?

Digital Resources

Solve   Learn   Glossary

Tools   Assessment   Help   Games

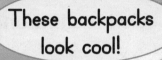

These backpacks look cool!

But which one would work better for you?

Wow! Let's do this project and learn more.

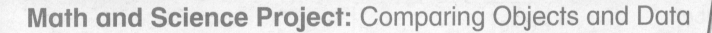

Math and Science Project: Comparing Objects and Data

Find Out Work with a partner. Compare two backpacks. Which one holds more? Which one has more parts? Which one is easier to put on? Think of other ways to compare.

Journal: Make a Book Show what you learn in a book. In your book, also:

• Tell one good thing and one bad thing about each backpack.

• Draw line plots, picture graphs, and bar graphs to show and compare data.

Name _____

Review What You Know

A-Z Vocabulary

1. Circle the number that has a 6 in the **tens** place.

406

651

160

2. Circle the **tally marks** that show 6.

Favorite Toy	
Car	$\cancel{||||}\ ||$
Blocks	$||||$
Doll	$\cancel{||||}\ |$

3. Circle the **difference**.

$22 - 9 = 13$

$34 + 61 = 95$

Comparing Numbers

4. A zoo has 405 snakes. It has 375 monkeys. Compare the number of snakes to the number of monkeys.

Write > or <.

405 ◯ 375

Interpret Data

5.

Picnic Tickets Sold	
Jean	16
Paulo	18
Fatima	12

Who sold the most picnic tickets?

_____

Addition and Subtraction

6. Byron scores 24 points in a game. Ava scores 16 points in the same game. How many more points does Byron score than Ava?

_____ more points

---

800 eight hundred

Topic 14

My Word Cards

Study the words on the front of the card.
Complete the activity on the back.

A-Z
Glossary

data

Favorite Fruit

Apple	7
Peach	4
Orange	5

line plot

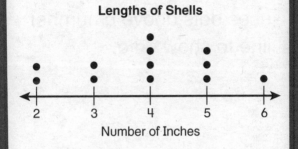

Lengths of Shells

Number of Inches

bar graph

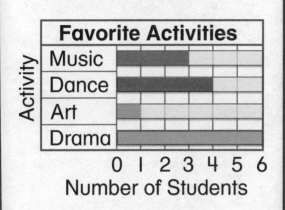

Favorite Activities

Activity: Music, Dance, Art, Drama

0 1 2 3 4 5 6
Number of Students

symbol

A 𝑖 stands for 1 student.
Some math symbols: = + −

picture graph

Favorite Ball Games

Baseball	𝑖 𝑖
Soccer	𝑖 𝑖 𝑖 𝑖 𝑖 𝑖 𝑖 𝑖
Tennis	𝑖 𝑖 𝑖 𝑖

Each 𝑖 = 1 student

My Word Cards

Use what you know to complete the sentences.
Extend learning by writing your own sentence using each word.

A _____

uses bars to show data.

A _____

uses dots above a number line to show data.

_____

are information you collect.

A _____

_____

uses pictures to show data.

A _____

is a picture or character that stands for something.

Solve

Lesson 14-1
Line Plots

Solve & Share

Find four objects that are each shorter than 9 inches. Measure the length of each object to the nearest inch. Record the measurements in the table.

Then plot the data on the number line.

Which object is longest? Which is shortest?

I can ...
measure the lengths of objects, then make a line plot to organize the data.

I can also use math tools correctly.

Object	Length in Inches

Lengths of Objects

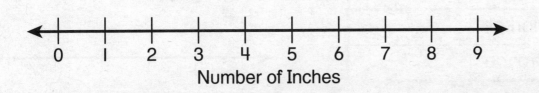

Number of Inches

2 inches long

You can measure the length of objects. This large glue stick is 2 inches long.

You can use a table to record the measurement **data**.

Object	Length in Inches
Glue stick	2
String	4
Feather	6
Scissors	4

You can make a **line plot** to show the data. Place a dot over the number that shows each length.

The two dots above the 4 tell me that two objects are 4 inches long.

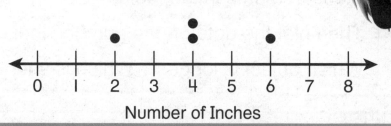

Lengths of Objects

Number of Inches

Do You Understand?

Show Me! Measure the length of your pencil to the nearest inch. Record your measurement on the line plot above. How does it change the data?

⭐ **Guided Practice** ⭐ Measure each object in inches. Record each length in the table. Then make a line plot. Show each length on the line plot.

1. ___4___ inches long

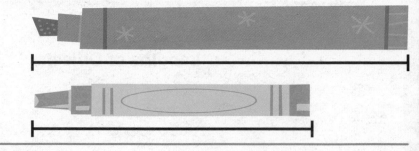

_____ inches long

2.

Object	Length (in.)
Marker	4
Crayon	

Lengths of Objects

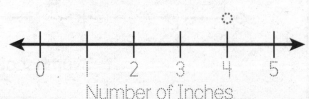

Number of Inches

Name _____

Independent ⭐ Practice

Measure each object in inches. Record each length in the table. Show each length on the line plot.

3. The paintbrush is _____ inches long.

4. The chalk is _____ inches long.

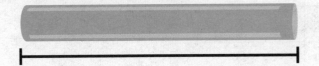

5. The straw is _____ inches long.

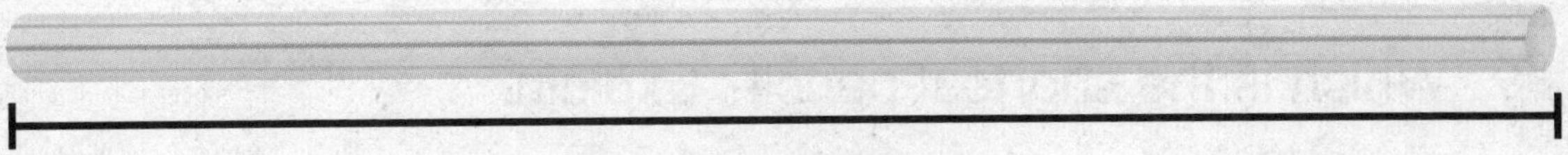

6. The glue stick is _____ inches long.

7.

Object	Length in Inches
Paintbrush	
Chalk	
Straw	
Glue Stick	

Lengths of Objects

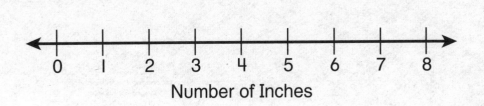

Number of Inches

8. **Model** Sophia measured the length of her colored pencils and made a table. Use the data to make a line plot.

Pencil Color	Length in Inches
Red	4
Blue	3
Green	7
Yellow	9

A line plot can help you make sense of the data.

Lengths of Pencils

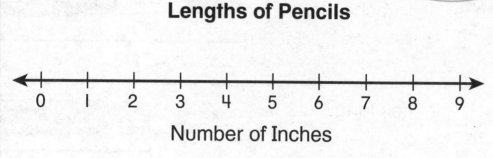

Number of Inches

9. Which is the shortest pencil? Explain.

_____

_____

10. **Higher Order Thinking** Which two pencils have a total length of 16 inches? Explain.

_____

_____

_____

11. ✓**Assessment** Measure the length of the purple pencil in inches. Write the length below. Record your measurement on the line plot above in Item 8.

_____ inches

Name _____

Another Look! You can make a line plot to show data.

The table shows the lengths of objects in inches.
Use the data from the table to make a line plot.

HOME ACTIVITY Use the line plot to ask your child questions about the data. Encourage your child to explain each answer.

Object	Length in Inches
Pencil	5
Scissors	8
Stapler	6

Lengths of Objects

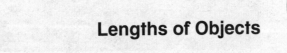

Number of Inches

The line plot helps you see which object is shortest and which one is longest.

 Use the line plot above to answer the questions.

1. Which object is longest? _____

2. Which object is shortest? _____

3. How much shorter is the stapler than the scissors? _____

4. How much longer is the scissors than the pencil? _____

Be Precise Measure each shoe in inches. Then record each length in the table. Show each length on the line plot.

5. The green shoe is _____ long.

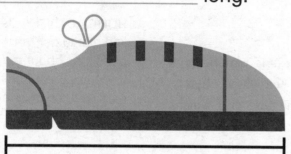

6. The purple shoe is _____ long.

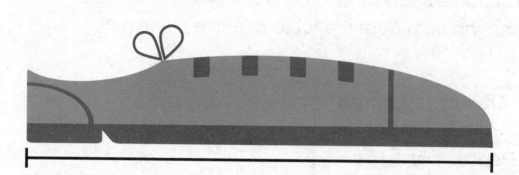

7.

Shoe Color	Length in Inches
Blue	4
Red	5
Green	
Purple	

Lengths of Shoes

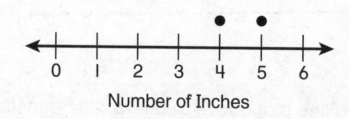

Number of Inches

8. Higher Order Thinking Which three shoes have a total length of 13 inches? Explain.

_____

_____

9. ✓**Assessment** Measure the length of the yellow shoe in inches. Write the length below. Record your measurement on the line plot above.

_____

Name _____

★ ☆ ★
Solve & Share

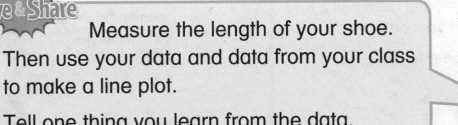

Measure the length of your shoe. Then use your data and data from your class to make a line plot.

Tell one thing you learn from the data.

Lesson 14-2
More Line Plots

I can ...
measure the lengths of objects, then make a line plot to organize the data

I can also be precise in my work.

Shoe Lengths

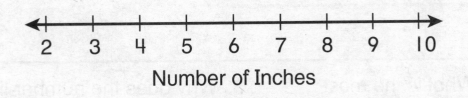

2 3 4 5 6 7 8 9 10

Number of Inches

Topic 14 | Lesson 2

Digital Resources at SavvasRealize.com

eight hundred nine **809**

Some students measure their heights. They record the data in a table. Are there any patterns in the data?

Student Heights in Inches

46	48	47	49
49	47	46	48
48	49	50	47
49	48	49	51

You can make a line plot to look for patterns.

To make a line plot, draw a number line, and write a title and labels to fit your data.

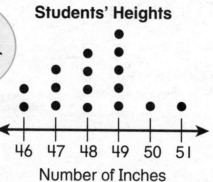

Students' Heights

Number of Inches

The most common height is 49 inches tall!

A line plot helps you organize data.

What else does the data show?

Do You Understand?

Show Me! How many students measured their height? Tell how you know.

☆ **Guided Practice** ☆ Use the table to make a line plot. Then use the line plot to answer each question.

1.

Feather Lengths (cm)

7	5	6	4
9	4	7	6
6	8	6	4
7	5	8	6

Feather Lengths

Number of Centimeters

2. What is the most common feather length? _6_ cm

3. Why does the number line use the numbers 4 through 9?

_____

_____

Topic 14 | Lesson 2

Independent Practice

Collect data and use the data to complete the line plot. Then use the line plot to solve the problems.

4. Measure the length of your pencil in centimeters. Collect pencil-length data from your classmates. Make a line plot with the data.

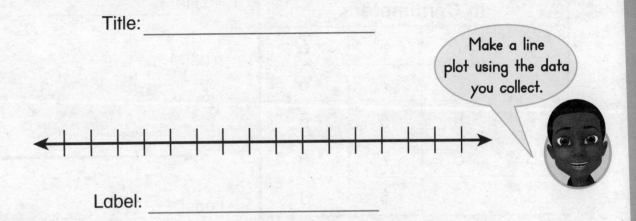

Title: _____

Label: _____

Make a line plot using the data you collect.

---

5. What is the length of the longest pencil?

_____

6. What is the length of the shortest pencil?

_____

---

7. What is the difference in length between the shortest and longest pencil?

_____

8. What is the most common pencil length?

_____

---

9. 🅐🅩 **Vocabulary** Use these words to complete the sentences.   **longest   line plot   order**

A _____ can help you see the data in _____.

A line plot makes it easy to see the shortest and _____ objects.

Model Use the data in the table to complete the line plot. Then use the line plot to solve the problems.

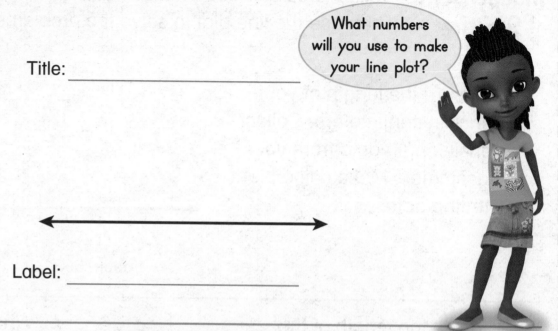

10.

Crayon Lengths in Centimeters			
6	7	5	6
7	5	7	6
7	8	6	5
5	6	7	6
8	8	6	8

Title: _____

What numbers will you use to make your line plot?

Label: _____

11. **Higher Order Thinking** How many crayons are longer than 5 centimeters? Explain.

_____

_____

_____

12. ✓**Assessment** Measure the length of the blue crayon to the nearest centimeter. Write the length below.

_____

Then record your measurement on the line plot above that you made in Item 10.

Name _____

Another Look! 7 students measured the length of the scissors to the nearest centimeter. The results are shown in the table below.

Length of Scissors in Centimeters			
8	7	7	6
7	6	7	7

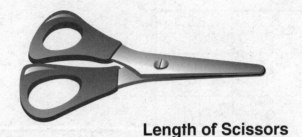

HOME ACTIVITY Have your child measure the lengths of three windows in your home. The windows should have different lengths. Then ask your child to make a line plot of the data.

Step 1 Measure the length of the scissors to the nearest centimeter.

Step 2 Write your measurement in the table above.

Step 3 Record your measurement on the line plot at the right.

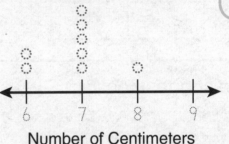

Length of Scissors

Number of Centimeters

Use the line plot above to answer each question.

1. Which measurement of the length of the scissors is most common?

   _____ centimeters

2. Why did people get different measurements? Write Yes or No.

   _____ The object has a shape that is **NOT** flat.

   _____ The measurement is halfway between two units.

   _____ The ruler is not aligned with 0 when used.

Model Measure the foot length of 3 friends or family members. Write the measurements in the table below. Then use the data to complete the line plot.

3.

Foot Lengths in Inches			
8	7	8	7
6	9	6	7
10	7	9	10
7			

Foot Lengths

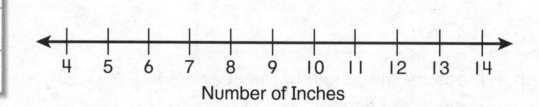

Number of Inches

---

4. How long is the shortest foot?

_____

5. What is the most common foot length?

_____

---

6. **Higher Order Thinking** How many people have a foot length that is an even number of inches? Explain.

_____

_____

_____

_____

7. ✓**Assessment** Measure the length of this foot to the nearest inch. Write the length below. Record your measurement on the line plot you made in Item 3.

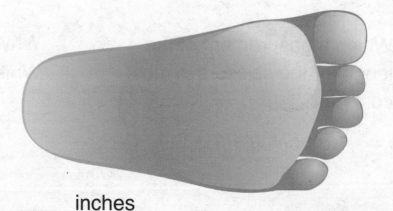

_____ inches

Solve & Share

The graph shows the number of birthdays in each season for a class.
How can you use the graph to write the number of birthdays in this table? Tell how you know.

I can ...
draw bar graphs and use them to solve problems.

I can also make sense of problems.

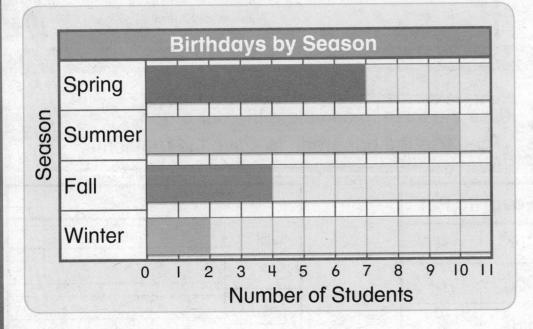

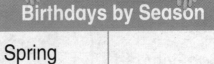

Birthdays by Season

Spring	
Summer	
Fall	
Winter	

Use the table to make a **bar graph**.
First, write a title and label the graph.

Then color boxes for each
activity to match the data.

> The length of the bars tell you how many students like each activity.

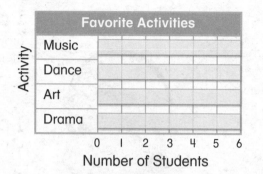

Favorite Activities	
Music	3
Dance	4
Art	1
Drama	6

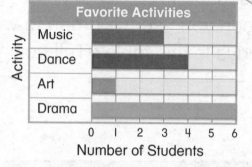

Favorite Activities	
Music	3
Dance	4
Art	1
Drama	6

Do You Understand?

Show Me! Which activity did the most students choose? Explain how you know.

☆ **Guided Practice** ☆ Use the table to complete the bar graph. Then use the bar graph to solve the problems.

Favorite Pet	
Cat	4
Dog	6
Bird	2
Turtle	3

Favorite Pet

1. How many students chose cat?

2. Which pet did the most students choose?

Name _____

Independent Practice ☆ Use the bar graph to solve the problems.

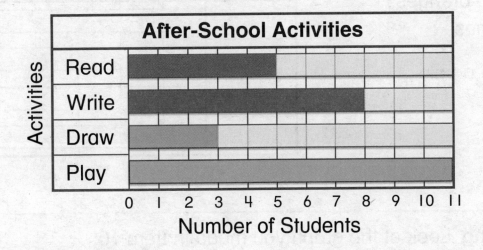

After-School Activities

Activities: Read, Write, Draw, Play
Number of Students

3. How many students write after school?

   _____

4. Which activity do exactly 5 students do after school? _____

5. Which activity do the fewest students do after school? _____

6. How many students read or draw after school? _____

7. Which activity do the most students do after school? _____

8. How many more students play than read after school? _____

9. **Higher Order Thinking** How would the graph be different if 2 students changed their after-school activity from Play to Read?

Problem Solving ☆ Solve the problems below.

10. **Model** Wanda went to the farm. She bought 8 pears, 5 oranges, 2 apples, and 9 peaches.

    Use this data to make a bar graph.

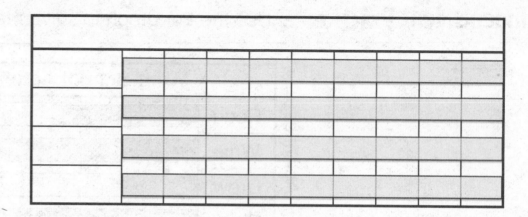

11. **Higher Order Thinking** Look at the graph you made in Item 10. How would the graph change if Wanda bought 3 more pears?

12. ✓**Assessment** Look at the bar graph you made in Item 10. Which is correct? Choose all that apply.

    ☐ Wanda bought the same number of pears and peaches.

    ☐ Wanda bought 3 more oranges than apples.

    ☐ Wanda bought 24 pieces of fruit in all.

    ☐ Wanda bought 4 more peaches than oranges.

Name _____

Help   Tools   Games

Another Look! The table shows how students voted to name the class goldfish.

Use the data from the table to make a bar graph.

Goldfish Names	
Flash	5
Goldie	3
Rocky	6
Bubbles	8

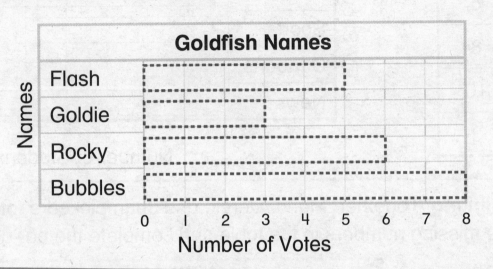

Goldfish Names

Names

Flash
Goldie
Rocky
Bubbles

0 1 2 3 4 5 6 7 8
Number of Votes

HOME ACTIVITY Gather three small groups of objects, such as 3 pens, 4 rubber bands, and 6 buttons. Make a table and a bar graph with your child to show how many of each object you have.

Use the bar graph above to solve the problems.

1. How many students voted for the name Goldie or the name Rocky?

_____

2. How many fewer students voted for the name Flash than voted for the name Rocky?

_____

3. Which name did the most students vote for? _____

4. Which name did the fewest students vote for? _____

Complete the bar graphs and solve the problems.

5. **Model** Use the data in the table to complete the bar graph.

Favorite TV Shows	
Animals	6
Sports	8
Cartoons	10
News	3

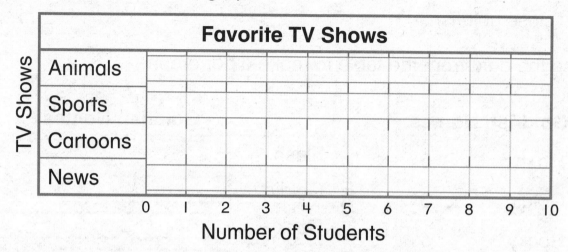

6. **Higher Order Thinking** Together, Marla, Derek, and Juan picked a total of 19 apples. Write the possible missing numbers in the table and complete the bar graph.

Apple Picking	
Marla	3
Derek	
Juan	

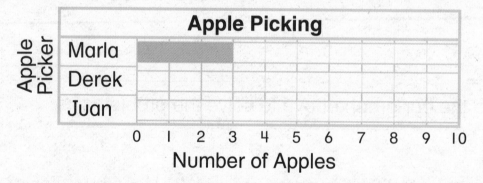

7. ✓**Assessment** Look at the bar graph in Item 5. Which statements are correct? Choose all that apply.

☐ 2 fewer students chose sports than animals.

☐ 10 students chose news or animals.

☐ 5 more students chose sports than news.

☐ 27 students in all were counted.

Name _____

Solve & Share

The graph shows the favorite subjects for a class. How can you use the graph to write the data in this table? Tell how you know.

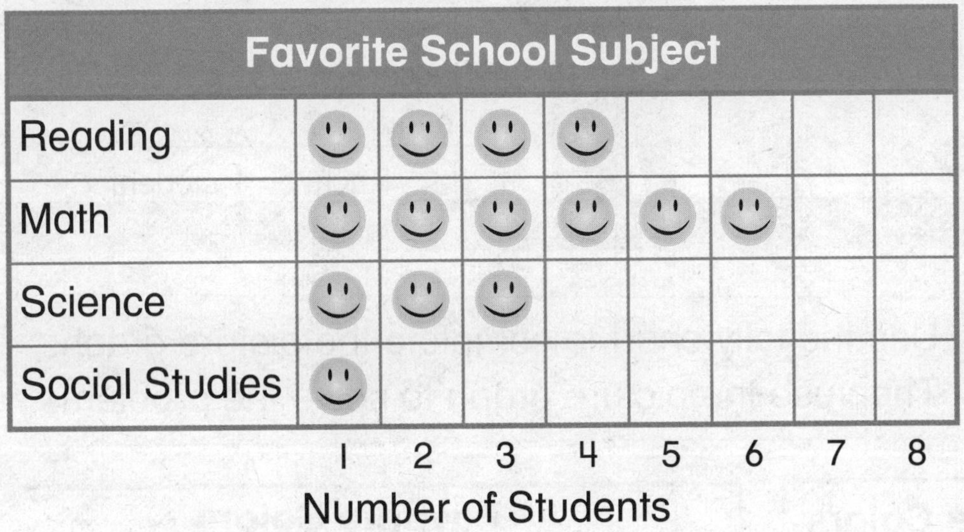

I can ...
draw picture graphs and use them to solve problems.

I can also model with math.

Favorite School Subject

	1	2	3	4	5	6	7	8
Reading	☺	☺	☺	☺				
Math	☺	☺	☺	☺	☺	☺		
Science	☺	☺	☺					
Social Studies	☺							

Number of Students

Favorite School Subject

Reading	
Math	
Science	
Social Studies	

Reading

Math

Learn Glossary

The tally chart shows the favorite ball games of Ms. Green's class.

Favorite Ball Games	
Baseball	II
Soccer	ℍ̶Ⅼ IIII
Tennis	IIII

You can show the same data in another way.

Choose a **symbol** to represent the data.

The symbol will be ⚲. Each ⚲ represents 1 student.

A **picture graph** uses pictures to show data.

You can draw the symbols to show the data.

8 students chose soccer!

Favorite Ball Games	
Baseball	⚲ ⚲
Soccer	⚲ ⚲ ⚲ ⚲ ⚲ ⚲ ⚲ ⚲
Tennis	⚲ ⚲ ⚲ ⚲

Each ⚲ = 1 student

Do You Understand?

Show Me! How are the tally chart and picture graph for the favorite ball games of Ms. Green's class alike?

★ **Guided Practice** ★ Use the tally chart to complete the picture graph. Then use the picture graph to solve the problems.

Favorite Colors	
Blue	ℍ̶Ⅼ
Red	ℍ̶Ⅼ I
Purple	III

Favorite Colors	
Blue	\ \ \ \ \
Red	
Purple	

Each 🖊 = 1 vote

1. How many students like blue best?

    5

2. Which color is the favorite of most students?

    _____

Name _____

Independent Practice Use the tally chart to complete the picture graph.
Then use the picture graph to solve the problems.

3.

Favorite Season	
Spring	IIII
Summer	ᵗʰˡ ᵗʰˡ
Fall	ᵗʰˡ I
Winter	II

Favorite Season	
Spring	
Summer	
Fall	
Winter	

Each 🧍 = 1 vote

4. How many students like fall best?

_____

5. Which season do exactly 4 students like best? _____

6. Which season do the fewest students like?

_____

7. How many students like the season with the fewest votes? _____

8. Which season do the most students like?

_____

9. How many students like the season with the most votes? _____

10. **Higher Order Thinking** Look at the picture graph above. How would the graph change if 2 students changed their votes from Summer to Fall?

_____

_____

Topic 14 | Lesson 4

eight hundred twenty-three **823**

11. **Model** Bob made a tally chart to show the trees in a park.

Trees in the Park	
Birch	III
Oak	THLI
Maple	THL
Pine	II

Trees in the Park	
Birch	
Oak	
Maple	
Pine	

Each 🎄 = 1 tree

You can model data using a picture graph.

12. **Math and Science** Birch, oak, maple, and pine trees are common in North America. Which type of tree is most common in the park? _____

13. **Higher Order Thinking** How many birch and maple trees are there in all?

_____

14. ✓**Assessment** Draw a picture graph to show the data in the table.

Favorite Drink	
Milk	III
Juice	IIII
Water	I

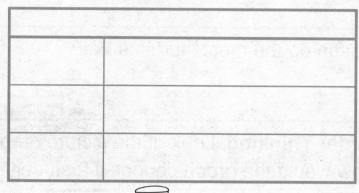

Each 🥤 = 1 vote

824 eight hundred twenty-four

Topic 14 | Lesson 4

Name _____

Another Look! A picture graph uses pictures or symbols to show information.

The number at the right tells how many students chose each snack. Complete the picture graph.

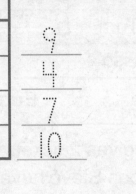

There are 9 symbols for popcorn. So 9 students chose popcorn.

HOME ACTIVITY Tell your child which snack shown in the picture graph is your favorite. Ask him or her to explain how the Favorite Snacks picture graph would change if your response was added to the picture graph.

Favorite Snacks		
Popcorn	☺☺☺☺☺☺☺☺☺	9
Fruit Cup	☺☺☺☺	4
Yogurt	☺☺☺☺☺☺☺	7
Cheese and Crackers	☺☺☺☺☺☺☺☺☺☺	10

Each ☺ = 1 student

Use the picture graph above to solve the problems.

1. How many students like cheese and crackers best?

_____

2. How many students like yogurt best?

3. Which snack is the least favorite?

_____

4. Which snack is most students' favorite?

_____

Solve each problem.

5. **Model** The tally chart shows how many tickets each student has. Use the tally chart to complete the picture graph.

Tickets We Have	
Denise	IIII
Steve	II
Tom	THL IIII
Lisa	THL I

Tickets We Have	
Denise	
Steve	
Tom	
Lisa	

Each 🎟️TICKET = 1 ticket

6. **Higher Order Thinking** Lisa gives 2 tickets to Steve. How many tickets does Steve have now? Explain.

7. ✅**Assessment** The tally chart shows the favorite pets of a class of second graders. Use the tally chart to draw a picture graph.

Favorite Pets	
Cat	THL I
Dog	THL II
Fish	THL
Hamster	II

💜 = 1 Vote

Name _____

Solve & Share

7 students voted for Turtle as their favorite pond animal.
10 students voted for Frog. 4 students voted for Fish.
Make a picture graph to show the data.
Write two things you notice about the data.

I can ...
draw conclusions from graphs.

I can also model
with math.

Favorite Pond Animals

Turtle	
Frog	
Fish	

Each ★ = I vote

1. _____

2. _____

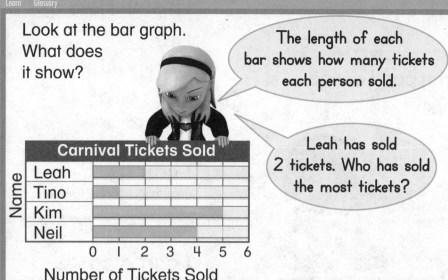

Look at the bar graph. What does it show?

The length of each bar shows how many tickets each person sold.

Leah has sold 2 tickets. Who has sold the most tickets?

You can also compare information and solve problems.

Kim sold the most tickets.

5 − 1 = 4
Kim sold 4 more tickets than Tino.

5 − 4 = 1
Neil sold 1 less ticket than Kim.

Do You Understand?

Show Me! Look at the graph above. How many tickets did Kim and Neil sell in all? How do you know?

☆ Guided Practice ☆ Use the bar graph to solve the problems.

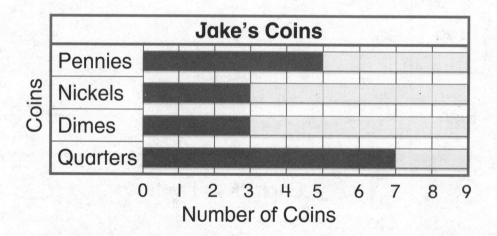

1. How many pennies does Jake have?

5

2. Jake spends 3 of his quarters. How many does he have left?

_____

828 eight hundred twenty-eight

Name _____

Independent Practice ☆ Use the bar graph to solve the problems.

3. How many students in all were absent on Tuesday and Thursday?

   _____

4. Were fewer students absent on Monday or Friday? How many fewer?

   _____

5. Three of the students absent on Friday were boys. How many girls were absent on Friday?

   _____

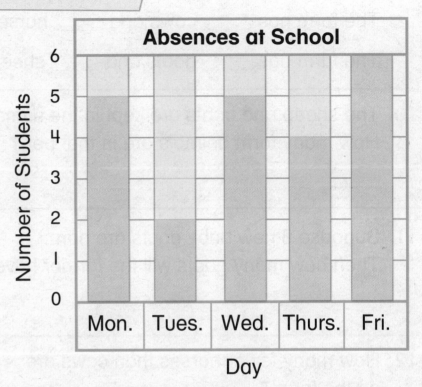

Absences at School

Number of Students

6
5
4
3
2
1
0

Mon. Tues. Wed. Thurs. Fri.

Day

6. On which two days were the same number of students absent?

   _____

7. Were more students absent on Wednesday or Thursday? How many more?

   _____

8. **Higher Order Thinking** The graph shows the number of students absent last week. This week, 19 students were absent. Compare the number of students absent this week to the number of students absent last week.

_____

_____

_____

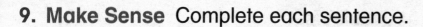

Problem Solving ☆   Use the bar graph to solve each problem.

9. **Make Sense** Complete each sentence.

The farm has _____ cows and _____ horses.

The farm has _____ goats and _____ sheep.

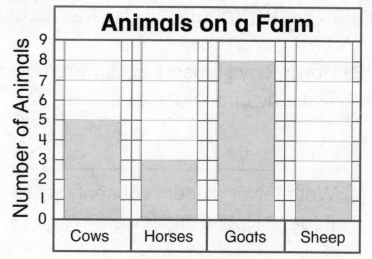

Animals on a Farm

10. The sheep and goats are kept in the same pen. How many farm animals are in that pen?

_____

11. Suppose 3 new baby goats are born. Then how many goats will the farmer have?

_____

12. How many fewer horses than cows are on the farm?

_____

13. Write the order of animals on the farm from the greatest number to the least number.

_____

14. **Higher Order Thinking** Do you think the bars on a bar graph should all be the same color? Explain.

_____

15. ✅**Assessment** The farmer wants to buy some sheep. He wants to have as many sheep as cows. How many more sheep should the farmer buy?

_____

     Topic 14 | Lesson 5

Name _____

Help Tools Games

Homework
& Practice 14-5
Draw
Conclusions
from Graphs

Another Look! You can draw conclusions from data in a graph.

This picture graph shows students'
favorite types of books.
Write how many students chose
each type of book.

The key shows that each book is 1 student's vote. Use the key to count the number of votes.

HOME ACTIVITY Use the Favorite Type of Book picture graph to ask your child questions about the data. Encourage your child to explain each answer.

Favorite Type of Book	
7	Biography
5	Adventure
4	Science
9	Mystery

Each 📕 = 1 vote

Use the picture graph above to answer the questions.

1. Which was the least favorite type of book?

_____

2. Which type of book did most students

vote for? _____

3. How many more students voted for
biography than for adventure?

4. If each student voted one time only, how
many students voted in all?

Use the bar graph to solve each problem.

5. Make Sense Complete each sentence.

The fruit basket has ＿＿＿ apples and ＿＿＿ pears.

The fruit basket has ＿＿＿ oranges and ＿＿＿ plums.

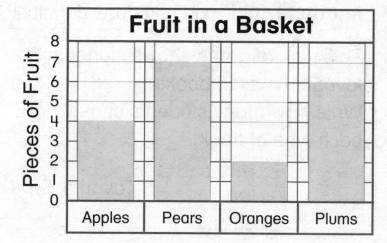

6. Write the order of the type of fruit from the least number to the greatest number.

＿＿＿＿＿＿＿＿＿＿＿＿＿＿＿＿＿

7. How many apples and oranges in all are in the basket?

＿＿＿

8. Maria uses 4 of the pears to make a pie. How many pears are left in the basket?

＿＿＿

9. **Higher Order Thinking** Does it matter how you order the data in a bar graph? Explain.

＿＿＿＿＿＿＿＿＿＿＿＿＿＿＿＿＿

＿＿＿＿＿＿＿＿＿＿＿＿＿＿＿＿＿

＿＿＿＿＿＿＿＿＿＿＿＿＿＿＿＿＿

10. ✅**Assessment** How many fewer apples than plums are in the basket?

＿＿＿

Name _____

Solve & Share

Make a picture graph to show how many connecting cubes, counters, and ones cubes you have. Then write and solve a problem about your data.

I can ...
reason about data in bar graphs and picture graphs to write and solve problems.

I can also add and subtract using data.

Math Tools	
Connecting Cubes	
Counters	
Ones Cubes	

Thinking Habits
What do the symbols mean?

How are the numbers in the problem related?

Each _____ = I math tool

_____

_____

_____

The bar graph shows the number of stamps each student has collected.

Write and solve a problem about the data in the bar graph.

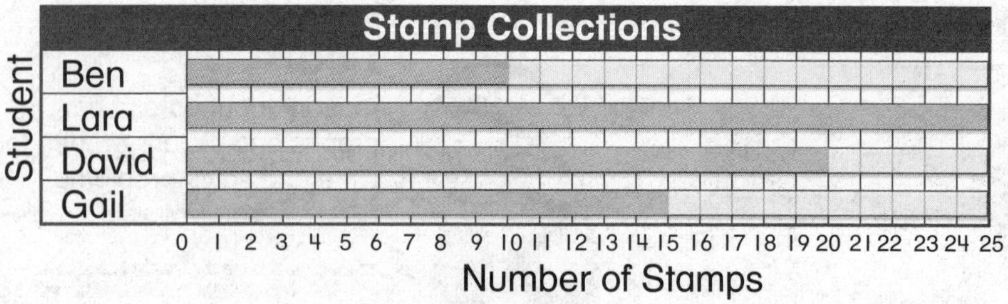

Stamp Collections

Student	
Ben	
Lara	
David	
Gail	

0 1 2 3 4 5 6 7 8 9 10 11 12 13 14 15 16 17 18 19 20 21 22 23 24 25

Number of Stamps

How can I use reasoning to write and solve a problem?

I can look at the bars to see how many stamps each student has.

I can write a problem to compare the number of stamps two students have.

My Problem

How many more stamps does Lara have than Gail?

25 – 15 = 10

10 more stamps

Do You Understand?

Show Me! Use reasoning to write your own problem about the data in the graph. Then solve it.

☆ **Guided Practice** ☆ Use the bar graph to write and solve problems.

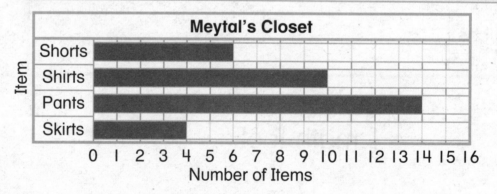

Meytal's Closet

Item	
Shorts	
Shirts	
Pants	
Skirts	

0 1 2 3 4 5 6 7 8 9 10 11 12 13 14 15 16

Number of Items

1. How many shirts and skirts are there in all?

10 $+$ 4 = 14

2. _____

___ ○ ___ = ___

Tools Assessment

Independent Practice ☆ Use the bar graph to write and solve problems.

3. _____

_____

_____

____ ◯ ____ = ____

_____

_____

_____

4. _____

_____

____ ◯ ____ = ____

_____

_____

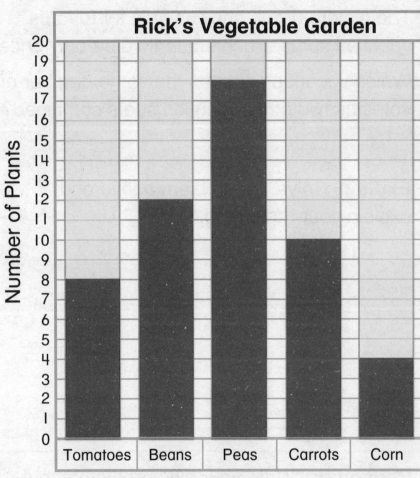

Rick's Vegetable Garden

(Bar graph — Number of Plants vs. Plants)

Plant	Number of Plants
Tomatoes	8
Beans	12
Peas	18
Carrots	10
Corn	4

Plants

Use reasoning to think about how the numbers, bars, and plants are related.

Problem Solving

Performance Assessment

Vacation Time!

The picture graph shows votes for favorite vacation spots. Each student voted only once.

Which vacation spot has the same number of votes as two other vacation spots combined?

Votes for Favorite Vacation Spot	
Beach	✓✓✓✓✓✓✓✓✓✓✓
Mountains	✓✓✓✓✓✓✓
City	✓✓✓✓
Theme Park	✓✓✓✓✓✓✓✓✓✓✓✓

Each ✓ = 1 vote

5. **Explain** Solve the problem above and explain your reasoning.

____

____

____

____

____

6. **Make Sense** How many students voted in all? Tell how you know.

____

____

____

____

____

7. **Reasoning** Write your own problem about the data in the graph. Then solve it.

____ ◯ ____ = ____

____

____

____

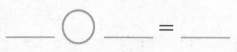

Name _____

Help   Tools   Games

Another Look! You can reason about data in the picture graph to write and solve problems.

How many more votes did the Tigers get than the Lions?

Count the symbols for the votes for Tigers and Lions on the picture graph. Then subtract.

Votes for Team Name	
Wolves	☺☺☺☺☺
Tigers	☺☺☺☺☺☺☺☺☺☺
Lions	☺☺☺☺☺☺☺☺

Each ☺ = 1 vote

HOME ACTIVITY Look at the picture graph for team names together. Ask your child to find how many more votes there are for Wolves and Lions combined than there are for Tigers. Have your child explain how to find the answer.

Tigers _10_   Lions _8_

_10_ – _8_ = _2_

The Tigers got _2_ more votes than the Lions.

Write and solve problems about the data in the picture graph above.

1. _____

_____

___ ◯ ___ = ___

2. _____

_____

___ ◯ ___ = ___

Gym Games

Ms. Winn has to cut one game from gym class. So, she asked students to choose their favorite game. The bar graph shows the results. Each student voted only once. Which game should she cut and why?

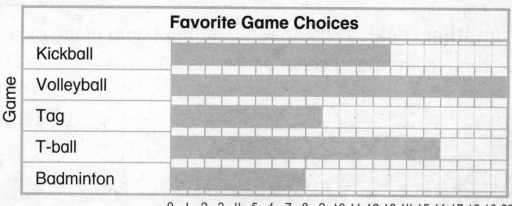

Favorite Game Choices

Game categories: Kickball, Volleyball, Tag, T-ball, Badminton

Number of Students: 0 1 2 3 4 5 6 7 8 9 10 11 12 13 14 15 16 17 18 19 20

3. **Make Sense** How many students voted for each game? Tell how you know.

_____

_____

_____

4. **Explain** Ms. Winn wants to cut tag from gym class. Do you agree? Explain.

_____

_____

_____

5. **Reasoning** How many fewer students chose tag and badminton combined than volleyball? Explain your reasoning.

_____

_____

_____

_____

Name _____

Find a Match

Find a partner. Point to a clue. Read the clue.

Look below the clues to find a match. Write the clue letter in the box next to the match.

Find a match for every clue.

I can …
add and subtract within 100.

Clues

A The difference is less than 16.

B The sum equals $43 + 25$.

C The difference equals $75 - 46$.

D The sum equals $53 + 20$.

E The difference equals $96 - 19$.

F The sum equals 75.

G The sum is between 60 and 65.

H The difference is between 25 and 28.

☐ 39 + 24	☐ 81 − 52	☐ 33 + 42	☐ 35 + 38
☐ 73 − 59	☐ 67 − 40	☐ 88 − 11	☐ 17 + 51

TOPIC 14 · Vocabulary Review

A-Z
Glossary

Word List
- bar graph
- data
- line plot
- picture graph
- symbol

Understand Vocabulary
Label each data display. Write *line plot, bar graph,* or *picture graph.*

1.

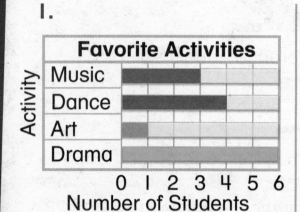

Favorite Activities

Activity	
Music	
Dance	
Art	
Drama	

0 1 2 3 4 5 6
Number of Students

_____

2.

Favorite Ball Games

Baseball	👥👥
Soccer	👥👥👥👥👥👥👥👥
Tennis	👥👥👥👥

Each 👤 = 1 student

_____

3.

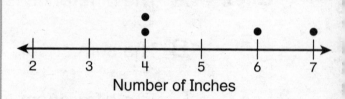

Lengths of Models

2   3   4   5   6   7
Number of Inches

_____

Use Vocabulary in Writing

4. Look at the graph in Item 2. Use words to tell how to find which ball game is the most popular. Use terms from the Word List.

_____

_____

_____

_____

_____

Name _____

Set A _____

Reteaching

Line plots show and organize data.
Use an inch ruler. Measure the length of
the toy car. Then record the measurement
in the table.

Complete the table and show
the data on a line plot.

1. Use an inch ruler. Measure the length of
the pencil. Then record the measurement
in the table.

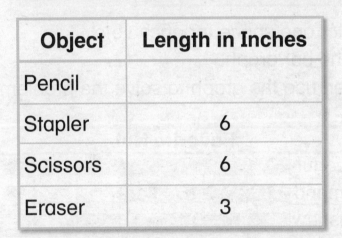

Toy	Length in Inches
Car	3
Airplane	5
Doll	5
Block	1

Object	Length in Inches
Pencil	
Stapler	6
Scissors	6
Eraser	3

Place a dot over the number that shows
the length of each toy.

2. Make a line plot to show each length.

Length of Toys

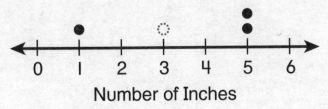

Number of Inches

Length of Objects

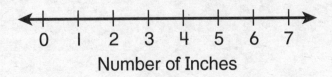

Number of Inches

Topic 14 | Reteaching

eight hundred forty-one **841**

You can make a bar graph to show the data in a table.

Students voted for their favorite nut. The table shows the number of votes.

Favorite Nut	
Peanut	7
Almond	4
Cashew	5

Color one space for each vote in the bar graph.

Then use the graph to solve the problem.

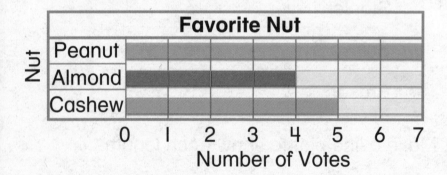

How many students voted? __16__

Use the table to complete the bar graph. Then solve each problem.

3.

Favorite Yogurt	
Lemon	3
Vanilla	7
Banana	6

4. How many more students voted for vanilla than banana? _____

5. How many fewer students voted for lemon than vanilla? _____

Set C _____

A picture graph uses pictures or symbols to show data.

The tally chart shows votes for favorite sea animals.

Favorite Sea Animals	
Whale	ⵏⵏⵏ I
Dolphin	II
Seal	IIII

Use the data to make a picture graph.
Each ⵣ stands for 1 vote.

Favorite Sea Animals	
Whale	ⵣⵣⵣⵣⵣⵣ
Dolphin	ⵣⵣ
Seal	ⵣⵣⵣⵣ

ⵣ = 1 vote

Which sea animal has the fewest votes?

dolphin

Use the tally chart to complete the picture graph.
Then solve each problem.

6.

Favorite Birds	
Blue Jay	ⵏⵏⵏ
Robin	ⵏⵏⵏ III
Seagull	ⵏⵏⵏ ⵏⵏⵏ

Favorite Birds	
Blue Jay	
Robin	
Seagull	

🐦 = 1 vote

7. How many votes did seagull get?

_____

8. Which bird had the fewest votes?

_____

Thinking Habits

Reasoning

What do the symbols mean?

How are the numbers in the problem related?

How can I write a word problem using the information that is given?

How do the numbers in my problem relate to each other?

How can I use a word problem to show what an equation means?

Use the picture graph to solve each problem. Each student voted once.

Favorite Winter Sport	
Skiing	❄❄❄❄❄❄❄
Snowboarding	❄❄❄❄❄❄❄❄❄❄
Skating	❄❄❄❄❄❄❄❄
Ice Fishing	❄❄❄❄

Each ❄ = I vote

9. How many fewer students chose ice fishing than snowboarding? _____

10. Write and solve your own problem about the data.

_____

_____

____ ◯ ____ = ____

Name _____

1. Pam has 5 pennies, 2 nickels, 8 dimes, and 9 quarters. Show this data in the bar graph below. Draw the bars.

Pam's Coin Collection

Coin

	Pennies
	Nickels
	Dimes
	Quarters

0 1 2 3 4 5 6 7 8 9 10

Number of Coins

2. Use the bar graph you made above. Pam spends 5 of her dimes to buy an apple. Now how many dimes does Pam have left?

Ⓐ 13

Ⓑ 5

Ⓒ 3

Ⓓ 0

3. Is each sentence about the picture graph correct? Choose Yes or No.

Favorite Camp Activity

Crafts	🧍 🧍 🧍
Swimming	🧍 🧍 🧍 🧍 🧍
Archery	🧍 🧍
Tennis	🧍 🧍 🧍 🧍 🧍 🧍

Each 🧍 = 1 camper

7 students voted for tennis. ○ Yes ○ No

16 students voted in all. ○ Yes ○ No

2 more students voted for swimming than for crafts. ○ Yes ○ No

3 fewer students voted for tennis than for crafts. ○ Yes ○ No

4. How many more tickets did Kendra sell than Leon?

(A) 5

(B) 6

(C) 11

(D) 17

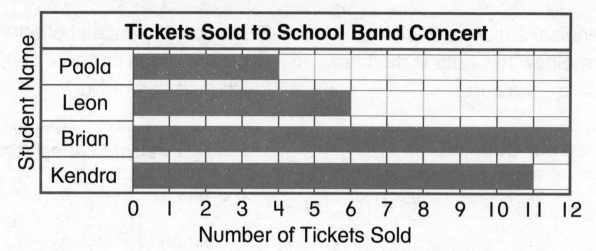

Tickets Sold to School Band Concert

Student Name: Paola, Leon, Brian, Kendra

Number of Tickets Sold: 0 1 2 3 4 5 6 7 8 9 10 11 12

---

5. Complete the table and the line plot.

Part A

Use a centimeter ruler. Measure the length of the crayon to the nearest centimeter. Write the length in the table below.

Crayon Lengths in Centimeters			
5	7	7	8
4	7	5	

Part B

Use the data in the table to complete the line plot.

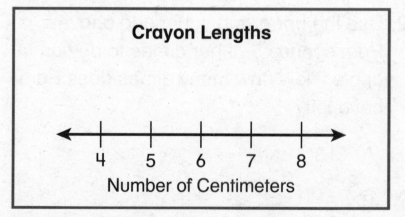

Crayon Lengths

4   5   6   7   8

Number of Centimeters

What is the difference in length between the shortest and longest crayon?

_____

6. Scott is making a picture graph from the data in the tally chart. How many symbols should he draw in the bottom row?

Favorite Fruit	
Apple	IIII
Banana	ⵘⵘ I
Pear	I
Orange	ⵘⵘ

Favorite Fruit	
Apple	😊 😊 😊 😊
Banana	😊 😊 😊 😊 😊 😊
Pear	😊
Orange	

Each 😊 = I student

Ⓐ 3   Ⓑ 4   Ⓒ 5   Ⓓ 6

---

7. Mary gets new stamps every month. The bar graph shows the number of stamps she collects each month.

Which statements are true? Choose all that apply.

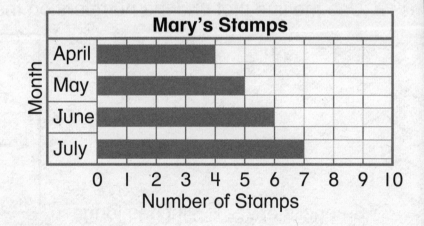

☐ Mary collects I more stamp in May than she does in April.

☐ Mary collects 2 fewer stamps in June than she does in July.

☐ Mary collects a total of II stamps in May and June.

☐ Mary collects one additional stamp each month from May to July.

---

8. Use the tally chart to complete the picture graph.
Then use the picture graph to solve the problems.

Favorite Flower	
Rose	卌 I
Daisy	III
Tulip	卌
Lily	卌 III

Favorite Flower	
Rose	
Daisy	
Tulip	
Lily	

Each 🌷 = I vote

How many students voted for Lily? _____

Which flower is the least favorite? _____

---

9. Use the line plot and the numbers on the cards to complete each sentence.

| 3 | 4 | 5 | 7 |

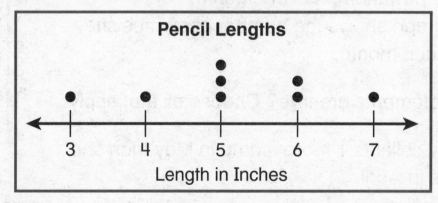

3 pencils are _____ inches long.

The longest pencil is _____ inches long.

The shortest pencil is _____ inches long.

The difference between the shortest and longest pencil is _____ inches.

Name _____

School Surveys

Some students asked their classmates different questions.

George asked his classmates to vote on their favorite lunch. This table shows the results.

Favorite Lunch	
Taco	5
Pizza	8
Hamburger	9
Salad	6

1. Use the table to complete the bar graph.

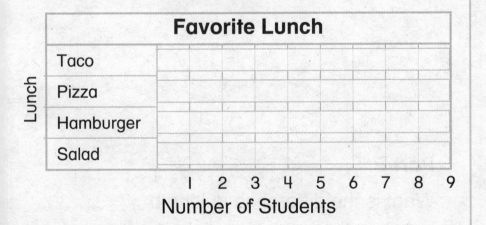

2. Use the Favorite Lunch table to complete the picture graph.

Favorite Lunch	
Taco	
Pizza	
Hamburger	
Salad	

Each ✔ = 1 student

3. Use the graphs you made to answer these questions.

How many students chose salad as their favorite lunch? _____

Which lunch is the favorite of the most students? _____

How would the bar graph change if two more students chose Taco?

_____

_____

4. Write and solve a math story about the Favorite Lunch graphs you made.

Part A

Use the bar graph or the picture graph about favorite lunches to write a math story problem. The problem should include addition or subtraction.

_____

_____

_____

Part B

Solve your math story problem. Explain how you solved the problem.

_____

_____

_____

5. Gina asked her classmates to measure the length of their favorite storybook in inches. She recorded their measurements in this table.

Lengths of Books in Inches			
12	9	8	10
6	10	11	9
10	9	9	12
12	10	7	7

Part A

Use the table to make a line plot.

Part B

What is the difference in length between the longest and shortest books?

_____ inches

Shapes and Their Attributes

Essential Question: How can shapes be described, compared, and broken into parts?

Digital Resources
Solve Learn Glossary
Tools Assessment Help Games

Different tools have different shapes!

How does the shape of a tool help it work?

Wow! Let's do this project and learn more.

Math and Science Project: All About Shape

Find Out Draw pictures of tools used for gardening, cooking, or fixing. Describe the shape of each tool. Tell how the shape of each tool helps it work.

Journal: Make a Book Show your work in a book. In your book, also:

• Choose a tool that you use at school. Tell how the shape of the tool helps it work.

• Draw and describe polygon shapes.

Name _____

Review What You Know

A-Z Vocabulary

1. Circle the shape that has 6 **sides**.

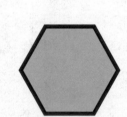

2. Circle each **plane shape**. Put a box around each **solid figure**.

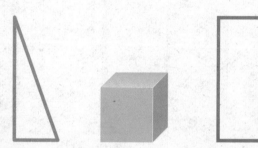

3. Put a box around the circle that shows **fourths**.

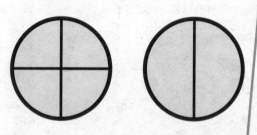

Basic Facts

4. Write each sum.

```
   5        7       10
 + 8      + 7     + 10
----      ----    ----
```

5. Write each difference.

```
  17       15       12
 - 9      - 6      - 8
----      ----     ----
```

Rectangles

6. Find the distance around.

```
    10 ft
  ┌────────┐
  │        │ 7 ft
  │        │
  └────────┘
```

_____

My Word Cards

Study the words on the front of the card.
Complete the activity on the back.

vertices (vertex)

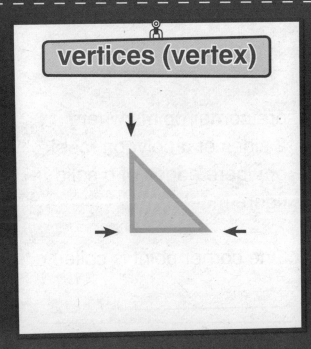

quadrilateral

pentagon

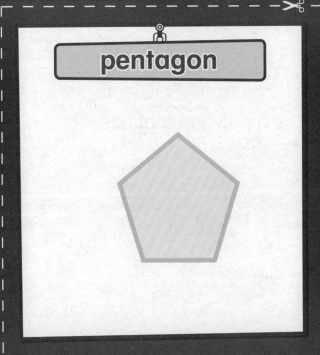

hexagon

polygon

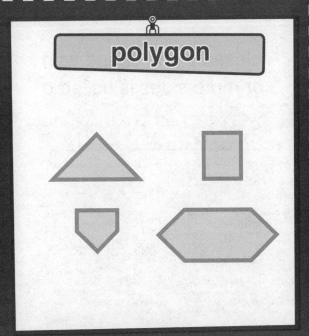

angle

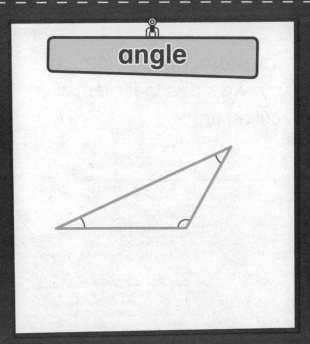

My Word Cards

Use what you know to complete the sentences.
Extend learning by writing your own sentence using each word.

A ______________________

is a polygon that has 5 sides.

A ______________________

is a polygon that has 4 sides.

____

are corner points where 2 sides of a polygon meet or where edges of a solid figure meet.

One corner point is called a

______________________.

The corner shape formed by two sides that meet is called an

______________________.

A closed plane shape with 3 or more sides is called a

______________________.

A ______________________

is a polygon that has 6 sides.

A-Z Glossary

My Word Cards

Study the words on the front of the card.
Complete the activity on the back.

right angle

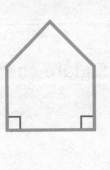

cube

face

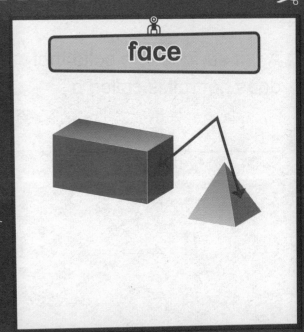

edge

equal shares

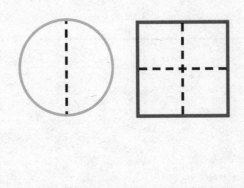

halves

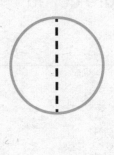

My Word Cards

Use what you know to complete the sentences.
Extend learning by writing your own sentence using each word.

A flat surface of a solid that does not roll is called a

_____.

A _____

is a solid figure with six faces that are matching squares.

A _____

_____

forms a square corner.

When a whole is divided into 2 equal shares, the shares are called

_____.

Parts of a whole that are the same size are called

_____.

A line formed where two faces of a solid figure meet is called an

_____.

My Word Cards

Study the words on the front of the card.
Complete the activity on the back.

A-Z
Glossary

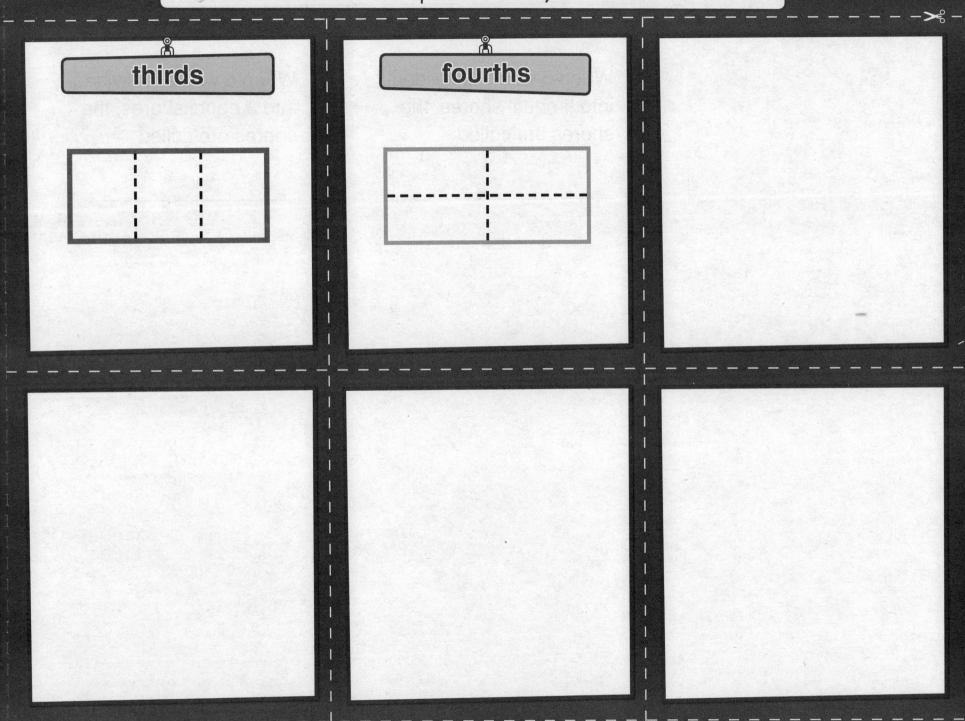

thirds

fourths

My Word Cards

Use what you know to complete the sentences.
Extend learning by writing your own sentence using each word.

When a whole is divided into 4 equal shares, the shares are called

_____.

When a whole is divided into 3 equal shares, the shares are called

_____.

Name _____

Solve & Share

Draw some closed plane shapes that have 3 vertices.
Write the name for one of your shapes.
Is this name correct for all of the shapes you made?

I can ...
recognize shapes by how they look.

I can also model with math.

3 vertices

Triangles

3 sides, 3 **vertices**

Not Triangles

Quadrilaterals

4 sides, 4 vertices

Not Quadrilaterals

Pentagons

5 sides, 5 vertices

Not Pentagons

Hexagons

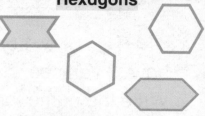

6 sides, 6 vertices

Not Hexagons

Do You Understand?

Show Me! How do sides and vertices help you name a plane shape?

Guided Practice Match each shape to its name.

1.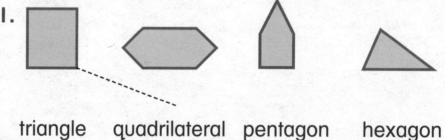

triangle   quadrilateral   pentagon   hexagon

Tell how many sides and vertices. Name each shape.

2.  _____ sides

_____ vertices

Shape: _____

3. _____ sides

_____ vertices

Shape: _____

860 eight hundred sixty

Topic 15 | Lesson 1

Name _____

Independent Practice   Match each shape to its name.

4.

triangle   quadrilateral   pentagon   hexagon

5.

triangle   quadrilateral   pentagon   hexagon

Draw the shape. Tell how many sides and vertices.

6. Quadrilateral

_____ sides

_____ vertices

7. Hexagon

_____ sides

_____ vertices

8. Triangle

_____ sides

_____ vertices

9. Higher Order Thinking Bianca drew a triangle and a pentagon.
How many sides and vertices did she draw in all? Draw the shapes.

_____ sides   _____ vertices

10. **Model** Marcos has 4 toothpicks. He places them as shown. What shape can Marcos make if he adds one more toothpick?

_____

11. A-Z **Vocabulary** Connect all the dots to make two shapes that have **vertices.** Name the shapes that you make.

• • •
• • •
• • • •

_____ _____

12. **Higher Order Thinking** Randall said that a square is a quadrilateral. Susan said that a square is a square, so it is not a quadrilateral. Who is correct? Explain.

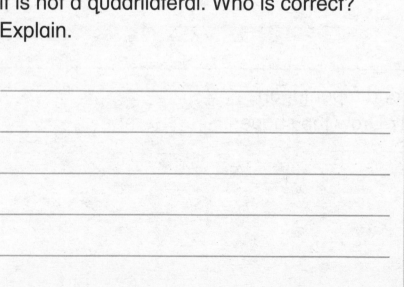

_____
_____
_____
_____
_____

13. ✓**Assessment** Which polygon is **NOT** a hexagon?

Ⓐ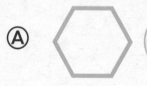

Ⓑ

Ⓒ

Ⓓ

Think: What do I know about hexagons?

Name _____

Another Look! You can name shapes by their number of sides and vertices.

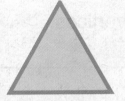 A triangle has
__3__ sides and
__3__ vertices.

 A quadrilateral has
__4__ sides and
__4__ vertices.

 A pentagon has
__5__ sides and
__5__ vertices.

 A hexagon has
__6__ sides and
__6__ vertices.

HOME ACTIVITY Look around your home for items that are shaped like triangles, quadrilaterals, pentagons, or hexagons. Ask your child to tell the number of sides and vertices for each shape.

 Name each shape.
Write the number of sides and vertices.

1.

Shape: _____

____ sides

____ vertices

2.

Shape: _____

____ sides

____ vertices

3.

Shape: _____

____ sides

____ vertices

Tell how many sides or vertices each student drew.

4. Algebra Leona drew 2 pentagons.

She drew _____ vertices.

5. Algebra Nestor drew 3 quadrilaterals.

He drew _____ sides.

6. Algebra Kip drew a hexagon and a triangle.

He drew _____ vertices.

7. Model Draw 2 hexagons that look different from the one shown.

8. Model Draw 2 quadrilaterals that look different from the one shown.

9. Higher Order Thinking Tami traced the flat sides of this wooden block. What shapes did she draw? Name and draw the shapes.

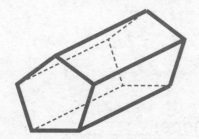

10. ✓**Assessment** Jin drew two polygons. One of the polygons is shown below. If Jin drew 9 sides and 9 vertices in all, which other polygon did he draw?

Ⓐ triangle   Ⓒ rectangle

Ⓑ rhombus   Ⓓ pentagon

Solve & Share

Look at the two plane shapes below. How are they alike? How are they different? What is a name for both shapes?

I can …
describe plane shapes by how they look.

I can also look for patterns.

_____
_____
_____
_____

Polygon

A closed plane shape with 3 or more sides is called a polygon.

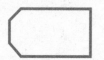
You know the names of these polygons.

Not Polygons

Polygons are not open shapes. Polygons do not have curved sides.

A circle is not a polygon.

Angle

Polygons have angles. They have the same number of angles as sides and vertices.

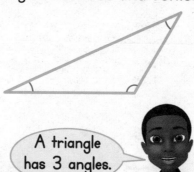

A triangle has 3 angles.

Right Angle

A right angle forms a square corner. A square has 4 right angles. The pentagon below has 2 right angles.

Do You Understand?

Show Me! How many angles does this shape have? How many right angles? Name the shape.

Guided Practice

Write the number of angles and then name the shape.

1.

_____ angles

Shape: _____

2.

_____ angles

Shape: _____

3.

_____ angles

Shape: _____

4.

_____ angles

Shape: _____

Tools   Assessment

Independent Practice   Write the number of angles and then name the shape.

5. 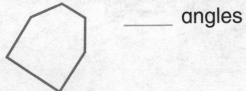 _____ angles

Shape: _____

6. _____ angles

Shape: _____

7.  _____ angles

Shape: _____

8. _____ angles

Shape: _____

9. _____ angles

Shape: _____

10. _____ angles

Shape: _____

11. Higher Order Thinking Draw a polygon with 2 right angles and 2 angles that are not right angles. Name the shape you draw.

How many angles will your polygon have in all?

12. Be Precise Which plane shapes are sewn together in the soccer ball?

13. Math and Science Bees make honeycomb. The honeycomb shape uses the least amount of wax. Name the shape. Tell how many angles the shape has.

14. Higher Order Thinking Draw a polygon shape that has 7 angles.
How many sides does the polygon have?
How many vertices does it have?

15. ✓**Assessment** Name the shape of the sign below. Write 3 things that describe the shape.

Name _____

Help   Tools   Games

Another Look! Polygons are closed plane shapes with 3 or more sides. Polygons have the same number of angles and vertices as sides.

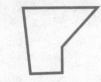

side

angle

vertex

An angle that forms a square corner is called a right angle.

Name and describe this polygon.

Pentagon   5 sides   5 vertices   5 angles

HOME ACTIVITY Ask your child to find objects that have polygon shapes. Have your child name each shape and tell how many angles it has.

Write the number of angles and then name the shape.

1. _____ angles

Shape: _____

2. _____ angles

Shape: _____

3. _____ angles

Shape: _____

Solve each problem.

4. Be Precise The sign below tells drivers to yield. This means to wait for other cars or people to go first.
Which polygon shape do you see in the sign?

_____

5. 🔤 Vocabulary The outside edges of this nut for a bolt form a **polygon** shape. Name that shape.

_____

6. Higher Order Thinking Look at the design below. Write three names for the shape that has right angles.

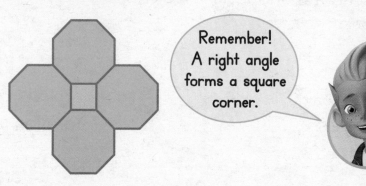

_____

7. ✔Assessment Name the shape below. Write 3 things that describe the shape.

Name _____

Solve & Share

Draw a polygon with 3 sides that are the same length. Then draw a polygon with 3 sides that are different lengths. Then tell 4 ways they are alike.

Sides: Same Length

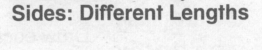
Sides: Different Lengths

_____

_____

_____

_____

Draw a polygon with 5 vertices.

My polygon will have 5 vertices. That means it will have 5 sides, too!

I drew a pentagon!

Draw a polygon with 4 sides that are the same length.

My next polygon will have 4 sides, so I will draw a quadrilateral! The sides should be the same length.

I drew a quadrilateral!

Do You Understand?

Show Me! Draw a quadrilateral with 4 sides that are the same length and with 4 right angles. Write 2 names for the quadrilateral.

☆ Guided Practice ☆ Draw each shape. Complete the sentences.

1. Draw a polygon with 3 vertices.

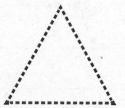

The polygon also has ____ sides.

The polygon is a

_____.

2. Draw a polygon with 6 sides.

The polygon also has ____ angles.

The polygon is a

_____.

Name _____

Independent Practice ☆ Draw each shape. Complete the sentences.

3. Draw a polygon with 3 vertices and 1 right angle.

The polygon also has

_____ sides.

The polygon is

a _____ .

4. Draw a quadrilateral with opposite sides that are the same length.

The polygon also has

_____ vertices.

The polygon is

a _____ .

5. Draw a polygon with 4 sides that are the same length.

The polygon also has

_____ angles.

The polygon is

a _____ .

6. Draw a polygon with 4 sides that are different lengths.

The polygon also has

_____ angles.

The polygon is

a _____ .

7. Draw a polygon with 5 vertices and 3 sides that are the same length.

The polygon also has

_____ sides in all.

The polygon is

a _____ .

8. **Higher Order Thinking** Can you draw a polygon with 3 vertices and 4 sides? Explain.

9. Be Precise Draw a rectangle with 4 equal sides.

What is another name for this shape?

_____

10. Draw 3 shapes. The first shape is a quadrilateral. The number of vertices in each shape increases by one.

Name the third shape. _____

11. Higher Order Thinking The owner of Joe's Fish Market wants a new sign. He wants the sign to have curved sides. Draw a sign for Joe's Fish Market.

Is the sign a polygon? Explain.

_____

_____

12. ✅ **Assessment** David drew two different polygons. One of the polygons was a square. If David drew 9 sides and 9 vertices in all, what other polygon did David draw?

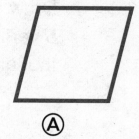
Ⓐ

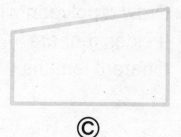
Ⓒ

Ⓑ

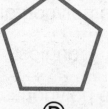
Ⓓ

Name _____

Another Look! The number of sides in a polygon is the same as the number of vertices and the number of angles.

Draw a polygon with 6 vertices.

The sides can be the same length.   The sides can be different lengths.

Each polygon has __6__ vertices.

Each polygon also has __6__ sides and __6__ angles.

Both polygons are __hexagons__.

 What pattern do you see?

Draw two different polygons for each number of vertices.

1. 4 vertices

Each polygon has _____ sides.

Both polygons are _____.

2. 5 vertices

Each polygon has _____ angles.

Both polygons are _____.

Draw each polygon. Then complete the sentences.

3. It has 2 fewer sides than a pentagon.

The shape is a _____.

4. It has 3 more vertices than a triangle.

The shape is a _____.

5. Make Sense It has 1 less vertex than a hexagon and 2 more angles than a triangle.

The shape is a _____.

6. Higher Order Thinking Tanika has 7 toothpicks. She uses them all to create two polygons. Draw two polygons that Tanika could have created. Write the names of your shapes.

7. ✅**Assessment** Kit drew a polygon that has 4 vertices. Which could **NOT** be Kit's polygon?

quadrilateral
Ⓐ

rectangle
Ⓒ

triangle
Ⓑ

square
Ⓓ

8. ✅**Assessment** Reg drew a polygon with more sides than a square and fewer vertices than a hexagon. Which could Reg have drawn?

triangle
Ⓐ

quadrilateral
Ⓒ

rectangle
Ⓑ

pentagon
Ⓓ

Name _____

Solve & Share

Describe this shape in 3 or more ways.

I can ...
draw cubes and describe how they look.

I can also be precise in my work.

A **cube** is a solid figure with 6 equal **faces**, 12 **edges**, and 8 vertices.

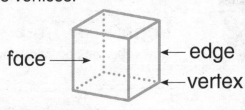

face ⟶

⟵ edge
⟵ vertex

Each face is a square, with 4 equal edges and 4 right angles.

These are cubes.

These are **NOT** cubes.

You can use dot paper to draw a cube. The dashed lines show the edges that you can't see when you look at a solid cube.

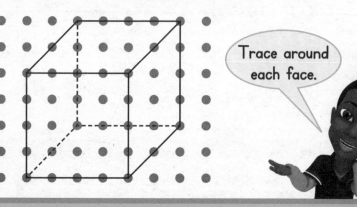

Trace around each face.

Do You Understand?

Show Me! What solid figure has 6 equal faces?

_____

What is the shape of each face?

_____

☆ Guided ☆ Practice

Circle the cubes in the group of shapes. Be ready to explain how you know they are cubes.

1.

2. Use the dot paper. Draw a cube.

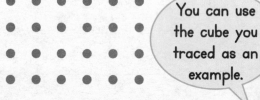

You can use the cube you traced as an example.

Tools Assessment

Independent Practice

Decide if the shape is a cube. Then draw a line from each shape to *cube* or **NOT** *a cube*.

3.

cube

NOT a cube

4. Trace the cube shown below.

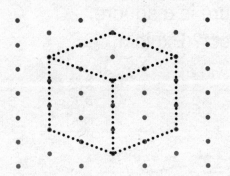

How many faces can you see?

_____ faces

Algebra Use what you know about cubes to write an equation and solve each problem.

5. How many vertices do these two cubes have in all?

____ + ____ = ____

_____ vertices

6. How many faces do these two cubes have in all?

____ + ____ = ____

_____ faces

7. **Explain** Scott is holding a solid figure with 6 equal faces, 12 edges, and 8 vertices. Scott says the figure is a cube. Carmen says the figure is a square. Who is correct? Explain.

_____

_____

_____

8. **A-Z Vocabulary** Circle the vocabulary word that completes the sentence.

vertices   **faces**   **edges**

A cube has 6 _____.

9. **Higher Order Thinking** Use a place-value ones cube or another solid cube. Look at the cube as you turn it. Turn the cube in any direction.

What is the greatest number of faces you can see at one time? Explain.

_____

_____

10. **✔Assessment** Complete the sentences about a cube.

A cube is a solid _____.

A cube has ____ equal faces,

____ vertices, and ____ edges.

Name _____

Another Look! You can tell if a shape is a cube by counting its faces, vertices, and edges. Number cubes are examples of real-life objects that are cubes.

Every cube has 6 equal square faces, 8 vertices, and 12 edges.

HOME ACTIVITY Have your child find an object at home that has a cube shape. Ask your child to describe the object including the number of faces, vertices, and edges.

These real-life objects are **NOT** cubes.

Tell whether each shape or object is a cube. If it is not a cube, tell what shape it is. Then explain how you know.

1. [ ] _____

_____

_____

_____

2. _____

_____

_____

_____

Use what you know about cubes to solve each problem.

This is another way to draw a cube.

3. **Look for Patterns** You can make two squares to draw a cube.

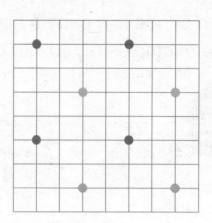

   1. Connect the 4 blue dots to make one square.
   2. Connect the 4 green dots to make another square.
   3. Connect each corner of the blue square to a like corner of the green square.

4. **Higher Order Thinking** Look at the solid figure below. Count the number of faces, vertices, and edges it has. Why is this figure **NOT** a cube?

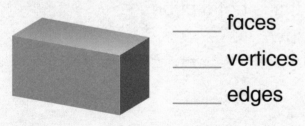

   _____ faces

   _____ vertices

   _____ edges

   _____

   _____

5. ✓**Assessment** Circle the shapes that are **NOT** cubes. Explain how you know.

   _____

Name _____

Solve & Share

How many equal squares cover this rectangle? How could you show this with an addition equation?

Columns

Rows

_____ equal squares

Equation: _____

How many red squares can cover this rectangle?

Begin like this:

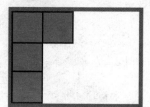

NOT like this:

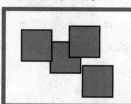

Count. Each row has 4 squares. You can add the squares by rows.

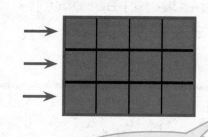

$4 + 4 + 4 = 12$

Count. Each column has 3 squares. You can add the squares by columns.

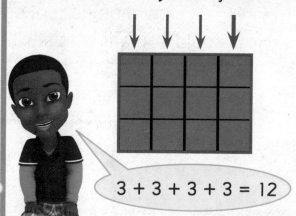

$3 + 3 + 3 + 3 = 12$

Do You Understand?

Show Me! Explain how you can divide a rectangle into equal squares.

☆ Guided Practice   Solve.

1. Use square tiles to cover the rectangle. Trace the tiles. Column 1 is done for you.

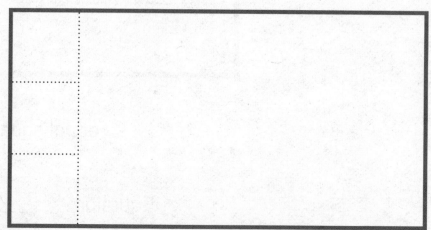

2. Count and add. How many squares cover the rectangle?

Add by rows: _____ + _____ + _____ = _____

Add by columns:

_____ + _____ + _____ + _____ + _____ + _____ = _____

884   eight hundred eighty-four

Independent Practice Use square tiles to cover each rectangle. Trace the tiles.
Count the squares.

3.

Add by rows:

____ + ____ + ____ + ____ = ____

Add by columns:

____ + ____ + ____ + ____ +

= ____

4.

Add by rows:

____ + ____ + ____ + ____ = ____

Add by columns:

____ + ____ + ____ + ____ = ____

5. **Number Sense** Draw a rectangle that is divided into
6 equal squares.

6. Look for Patterns Lisa bakes corn bread. She cuts it into equal square pieces. How many equal squares do you see? Write two equations to show the total number of square pieces.

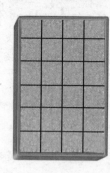

Rows: ____ + ____ + ____ + ____ + ____ + ____ = ____ pieces

Columns: ____ + ____ + ____ + ____ = ____ pieces

---

7. A-Z **Vocabulary** Label the **columns** and the **rows** for the large square below.

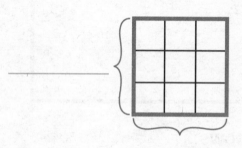

8. Higher Order Thinking Look at the large square in Item 7. What do you notice about the number of rows and the number of columns? Explain.

_____

_____

_____

_____

---

9. ✓**Assessment** Count the equal squares in the rows and columns of the rectangle. Then use the numbers on the cards to write the missing numbers in the equations.

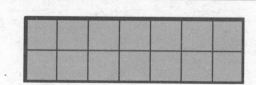

14	2	7

Rows: ____ + ____ = ____

Columns: ____ + ____ + ____ + ____ + ____ + ____ + ____ = ____

Name _____

Another Look! How many squares cover this rectangle?

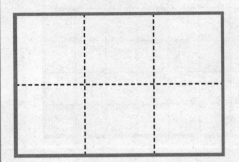

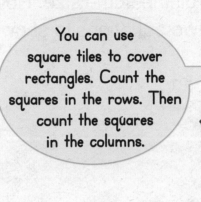
You can use square tiles to cover rectangles. Count the squares in the rows. Then count the squares in the columns.

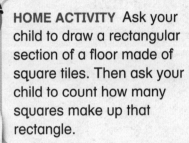

HOME ACTIVITY Ask your child to draw a rectangular section of a floor made of square tiles. Then ask your child to count how many squares make up that rectangle.

Add the rows: $3 + 3 = 6$

Add the columns: $2 + 2 + 2 = 6$

Use square tiles to cover the rectangle. Trace the tiles. Count the squares.

1.

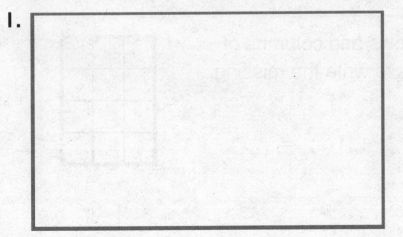

2. How many squares cover the rectangle?

Add by rows:

____ + ____ + ____ = ____

Add by columns:

____ + ____ + ____ + ____ + ____

= ____

Solve each problem.

3. **Look for Patterns** Mr. Cory puts square tiles on the kitchen floor. The square tiles are all the same size. How many equal squares are there? Write two equations to show the total number of square tiles.

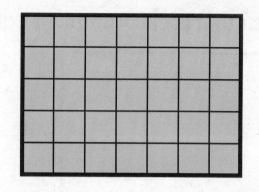

Rows:

_____ + _____ + _____ + _____ + _____ = _____ tiles

Columns:

_____ + _____ + _____ + _____ + _____ + _____ + _____ = _____ tiles

4. **Higher Order Thinking** 10 friends want to equally share a rectangular pan of granola bars. Show how to divide the rectangle into 10 equal pieces.

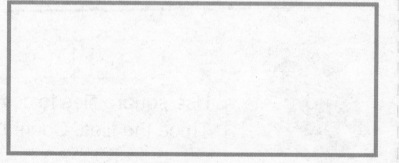

5. ✔**Assessment** Count the equal squares in the rows and columns of the rectangle. Then use the numbers on the cards to write the missing numbers in the equations.

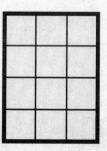

 4   12   3

Rows: _____ + _____ + _____ + _____ = _____

Columns: _____ + _____ + _____ = _____

Solve & Share

Use one type of pattern block to cover this shape.
Draw lines to show how you placed the pattern blocks.
How many equal shares does the shape have now?
What do you notice about the equal shares?

I can ...
divide circles and rectangles into halves, thirds, and fourths.

I can also look for things that repeat.

_____ shares

_____

_____

_____

Are these shares equal?	Are these shares equal?	Are these shares equal?	You can show equal shares in different ways.

2 equal shares | **NOT** equal shares

These shares are **halves**. | These shares are not halves.

3 equal shares | **NOT** equal shares

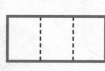 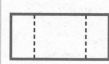

These shares are **thirds**. | These shares are not thirds.

4 equal shares | **NOT** equal shares

These shares are **fourths**. | These shares are not fourths.

Each share is a fourth of the square.

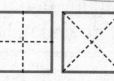

Do You Understand?

Show Me! Divide this rectangle into three equal shares. How many thirds is one share? How many thirds is the whole rectangle?

☆ Guided Practice Solve each problem.

1. Describe each equal share.
Write *a half of, a third of,* or *a fourth of*.

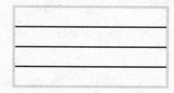

_____ _____ _____

2. Divide each square into halves. Show four different ways.

Topic 15 | Lesson 6

Independent Practice Divide each shape into the number of equal shares given. Show 2 ways. Then complete the sentences.

3. 3 equal shares

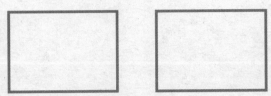

Each share is _____ the whole.

Each whole is _____.

4. 4 equal shares

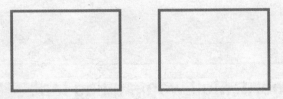

Each share is _____ the whole.

Each whole is _____.

5. 2 equal shares

Each share is _____ the whole.

Each whole is _____.

6. Higher Order Thinking Draw what comes next.

     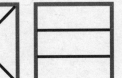

7. Model Leon cut a waffle into halves. Draw lines to show 3 different ways he could have cut the waffle.

8. Math and Science Tina is planting a garden. She wants to have equal parts for beans, for tomatoes, and for peppers. Draw a picture of how she could divide her garden.

9. Higher Order Thinking Draw lines on the picture to solve the problem.

4 friends want to share a watermelon. How could they cut the watermelon so each friend gets an equal share?

Each friend will get _____.

10. ✅**Assessment** Matt wants a flag that shows fourths. Which flags could Matt use? Choose all that apply.

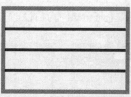 

Name _____

Another Look! Equal shares are the same size.

2 equal shares

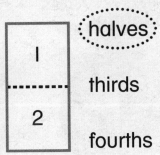

(halves)

thirds

fourths

3 equal shares

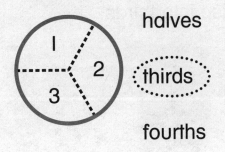

halves

(thirds)

fourths

4 equal shares

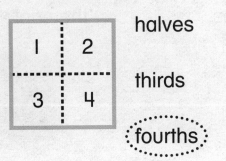

halves

thirds

(fourths)

HOME ACTIVITY Draw three squares. Ask your child to draw lines in one square to show halves. Then have your child draw lines in the second square to show thirds, and draw lines in the third square to show fourths.

Draw the number of equal shares given for each shape. Then circle the word that describes the shares.

1. 4 equal shares

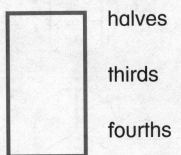

halves

thirds

fourths

2. 3 equal shares

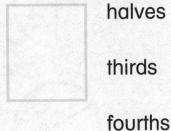

halves

thirds

fourths

3. 2 equal shares

halves

thirds

fourths

4. 4 equal shares

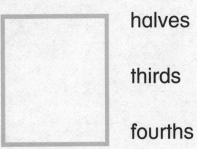

halves

thirds

fourths

Model Divide the shapes into equal shares.

5. Two students want to equally share a small pizza. Draw how to split the pizza into halves.

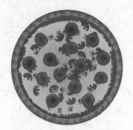

6. Three students want to equally share a tray of apple crisp. Draw two ways to split the apple crisp into thirds.

7. Four students want to share an apple pie. Draw lines to split the pie into fourths.

8. **Higher Order Thinking** This shape is divided into four pieces. Ryan says this shape is divided into fourths. Is he correct? Explain.

_____

_____

_____

9. ✓**Assessment** Tom cut his muffin in half to share it with his brother. Which pictures do **NOT** show halves? Choose all that apply.

☐ 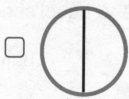   ☐

☐ 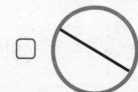   ☐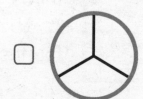

Name _____

⭐ **Solve & Share**

Divide this pizza into 4 equal shares. Compare your answer with a partner. Do you both have 4 equal shares? Did you both get the same answer?

I can ...
make equal shares that do not have the same shape.

I can also look for patterns.

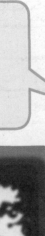

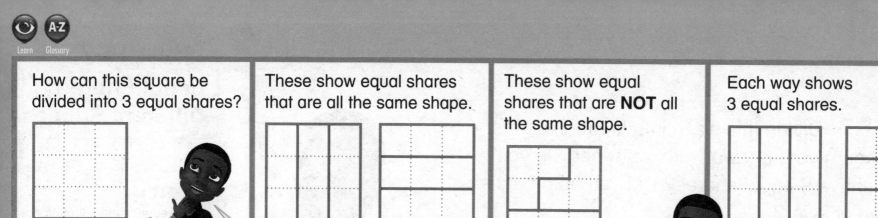

How can this square be divided into 3 equal shares?

You can use the smaller squares to help.

These show equal shares that are all the same shape.

You can draw lines to make 3 columns or 3 rows.

These show equal shares that are **NOT** all the same shape.

Each share is 3 squares. The shares are equal.

Each way shows 3 equal shares.

Equal shares can be different shapes.

Do You Understand?

Show Me! How can you check to make sure all of the shares are equal?

☆ **Guided Practice** ☆ Draw lines to show two different ways to divide the same rectangle into 2 equal shares.

1.

2. How many squares are in each equal share of the rectangles?

_____

3. Describe the equal shares and the whole.

Each share is ___a half of___ the whole.

Each whole is ___two halves___.

☆ **Independent**
☆ **Practice**
Draw lines to show two different ways to divide the same rectangle into 4 equal shares. Then answer the questions.

4. Show equal shares that are the **same shape**.   Show equal shares that are **different shapes**.

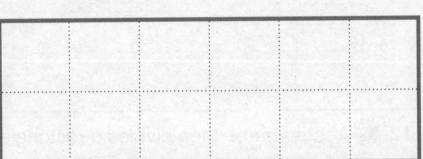   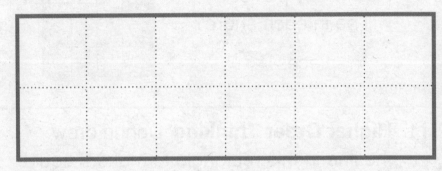

5. How many squares are in each equal share in Item 4? _____

6. Describe the equal shares and the whole in Item 4.

Each share is _____ the whole.

Each whole is _____ .

Draw lines to show two different ways to divide the same rectangle into 3 equal shares.

7.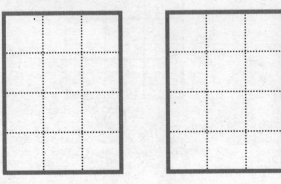

8. Higher Order Thinking How can equal shares in a rectangle have different shapes?

_____

_____

_____

9. Allen wants to share this pan of corn bread with 3 friends. Allen and his friends will each get an equal share.

How many pieces will be in each share?

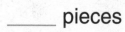 pieces

10. Explain Greg says that equal shares can be different in shape and size. Is Greg correct? Explain.

_____

_____

_____

11. Higher Order Thinking Donna drew the line in this rectangle to make 2 equal shares. Are the shares equal? Why or why not?

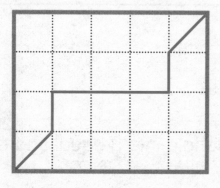

_____

_____

_____

12. ✅ **Assessment** Meg divides a rectangle into 3 equal shares that are **NOT** the same shape. Which could be Meg's rectangle?

Ⓐ

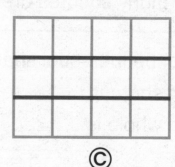

Ⓒ

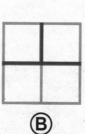

Ⓑ

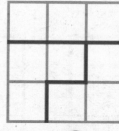

Ⓓ

Name _____

Help Tools Games

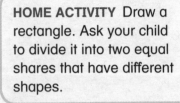

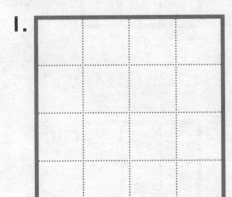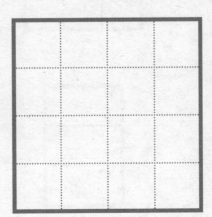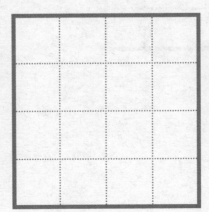

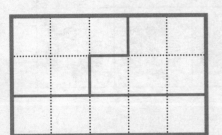

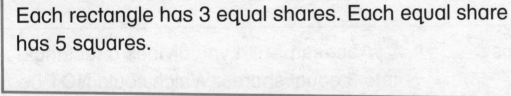

Another Look!

You can divide a rectangle into equal shares in different ways.

Each equal share has 5 squares.

Each rectangle has 3 equal shares. Each equal share has 5 squares.

HOME ACTIVITY Draw a rectangle. Ask your child to divide it into two equal shares that have different shapes.

Draw lines to show three different ways to divide the same rectangle into 2 equal shares.

1.

Can you divide a rectangle into equal shares that have DIFFERENT shapes?

Solve each problem.

2. **Explain** Lexi wants to share the sheet of tiger stickers with two friends. Are there enough stickers to make equal shares for Lexi and her two friends? Explain.

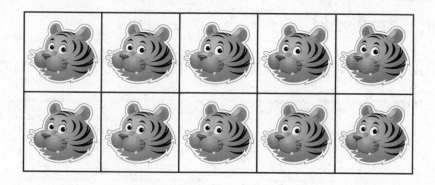

_____

_____

_____

3. **Higher Order Thinking** Corbin drew lines in this rectangle to make equal shares. How do you know that each share is **NOT** a third of the whole rectangle?

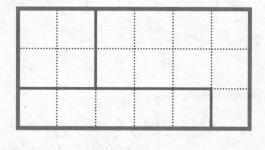

_____

_____

4. ✅**Assessment** Lynn divides a rectangle into 3 equal shares. Which could **NOT** be Lynn's rectangle?

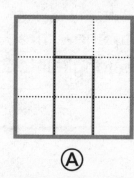

Ⓐ

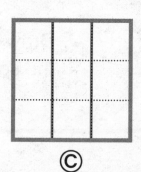

Ⓒ

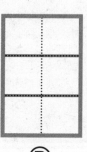

Ⓑ

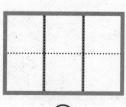

Ⓓ

Topic 15 | Lesson 7

Solve & Share

Design a flag made of 15 equal squares. Use rows and columns. Draw two possible flag designs. Then write an equation for each flag to show the total number of squares.

Divide each flag to make three equal shares. Color each share differently.

I can ...
use repeated reasoning to divide rectangles into rows and columns and to create designs with equal shares.

I can also use numbers and words to explain my work.

My Flag Designs

Equation:

Equation:

Thinking Habits
Does something repeat in the problem?

How can the solution help me solve another problem?

Sam is designing a square quilt. The quilt must have 4 colors with an equal share for each color.

Help Sam make two designs.

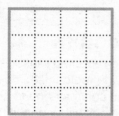

How can I look for things that repeat in the problem?

I can count the small squares in each share in my first design. That will help me draw the shares in my second design.

Here, I used the same shape for each share. Each share is 4 small squares.

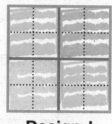

Design 1

In both designs, each colored share is one fourth of the whole.

Here, I used different shapes for the shares.

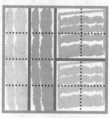

Design 2

Do You Understand?

Show Me! How do you know each share in Design 2 is a fourth of the whole square?

Guided Practice
Solve the problem. Use crayons to color.

1. Hamal is painting a design. The design must have 3 colors with an equal share for each color. Create two possible designs for Hamal.

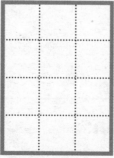

Design 1

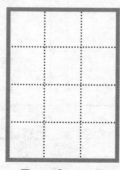

Design 2

Be ready to explain how you used repeated reasoning to help you solve the problem.

902 nine hundred two

Topic 15 | Lesson 8

Tools   Assessment

Independent Practice ✫ Solve each problem. Use crayons to color. Explain your work.

2. Marie wants to put a rectangular design on a T-shirt. The design must have 4 colors with an equal share for each color. Create two possible designs for Marie.

Design 1   **Design 2**

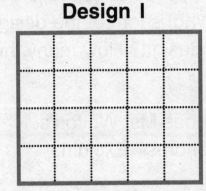 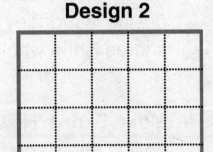

_____

_____

_____

3. Grant wants to put a circle design on his toy car. The design must have 3 colors with an equal share for each color. Create two possible designs for Grant.

Design 1   **Design 2**

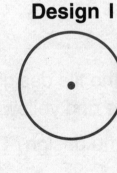 

_____

_____

_____

Problem Solving

Tile Design

Ms. Walton created this rectangular tile design. What share of the design is orange? What share of the design is yellow? How many shares is the whole design? How many thirds is the whole?

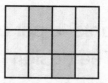

4. Make Sense How does Ms. Walton's design show equal shares? Explain.

_____

_____

_____

5. Reasoning What share of the design is orange? What share of the design is yellow? How many shares is the whole design? How many thirds is the whole?

_____

_____

_____

_____

6. Generalize Copy the tile design above onto this grid. Then color it orange and yellow to match the design shown above.

How did you copy the design? Describe one or two shortcuts you used.

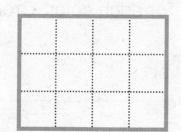

_____

_____

Name _____

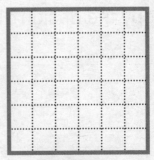

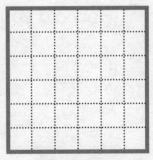

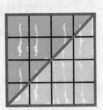

Another Look! Create two different designs for these squares that are the same size. Each design needs to have 2 colors with an equal share for each color.

I can draw a line down the center to make equal shares.

I can draw a line from opposite corners to make equal shares.

Design 2 also has equal shares that are the same shape.

Design 1

Design 2

HOME ACTIVITY Draw two identical rectangles. Have your child use crayons to draw a different design in each rectangle. Each rectangle should show 4 equal shares, each in a different color.

Solve the problem. Use crayons to color. Explain your solution.

1. Make two different designs. Each design must have 3 colors with an equal share for each color. One design should have shares that are NOT all the same shape.

_____

_____

_____

Design 1   **Design 2**

A Design Repeated

Steven created this design on 4 squares of grid paper.
He wants to repeat this design 6 times on a larger grid.
Answer the questions to help Steven create the larger design.

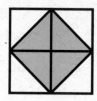

2. **Look for Patterns** Look at each small square of Steven's design. How are they alike? How are they different?

_____

_____

_____

3. **Explain** Describe Steven's design. Explain what it looks like. Use *half of, a third of*, or *a fourth of* when you describe it.

_____

_____

_____

4. **Generalize** Copy Steven's design 4 times.
Use 2 colors. Put 2 designs next to each other in each row.

How did you copy the design? Describe a shortcut you used.

_____

_____

_____

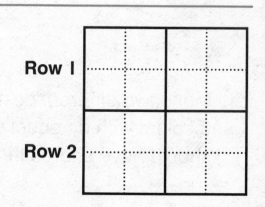

Row 1

Row 2

Name _____

Follow the Path

Find each sum or difference. Then color a path from **Start** to **Finish**. Follow the sums and differences that are even numbers. You can only move up, down, right, or left.

I can ...
add and subtract within 100.

Start								
69 − 23	31 + 25	78 − 47	97 − 49	72 + 12	76 − 38	67 − 47	48 + 24	46 + 37
84 − 61	73 − 55	68 + 29	11 + 17	37 + 58	86 − 51	21 + 38	82 − 18	81 − 62
43 + 42	27 + 49	35 + 48	46 − 32	73 − 26	30 + 31	46 − 28	47 + 41	62 − 39
25 + 16	60 − 36	50 − 29	39 + 43	60 − 45	64 + 23	29 + 35	56 + 41	94 − 61
35 + 42	85 − 23	24 + 56	58 + 36	97 − 38	25 − 16	38 + 62	79 − 49	59 + 23

Finish

Word List

- angle
- cube
- edge
- equal shares
- face
- fourths
- halves
- hexagon
- pentagon
- polygon
- quadrilateral
- right angle
- thirds
- vertex

A-Z Glossary

Understand Vocabulary

Write *always*, *sometimes*, or *never*.

1. A cube has exactly 4 faces. _____

2. A right angle forms a square corner. _____

3. Quadrilaterals are squares. _____

4. A solid figure with faces has edges. _____

Draw a line from each term to its example.

5. hexagon

6. pentagon

7. vertex

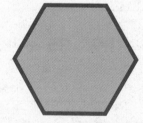

Use Vocabulary in Writing

8. Tell how you can divide a square into two equal shares. Then tell how you can divide that same square into 3 equal shares. Use terms from the Word List.

Name _____

Set A

You can name a plane shape by its number of sides and vertices.

vertex

side

3 sides

3 vertices

Shape: _triangle_

4 sides

4 vertices

Shape:

quadrilateral

Write the number of sides and vertices. Name the shape.

1.

_____ sides

_____ vertices

Shape: _____

2.

_____ sides

_____ vertices

Shape: _____

Set B

You can name a polygon by the number of its angles.

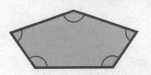

5 angles

pentagon

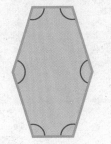

6 angles

hexagon

Write the number of angles. Then name the shape.

3.

_____ angles

Shape: _____

4.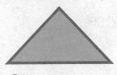

_____ angles

Shape: _____

You can draw a polygon with a given number of sides, vertices, or angles.

Draw a polygon with 4 sides that are different lengths.

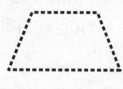

Draw a polygon with 5 vertices.

Draw a polygon with 3 angles. One angle is a right angle.

Draw each polygon described.

5. 6 sides

6. 3 vertices

7. 5 sides and 2 right angles

8. 8 angles

You can describe and draw cubes.

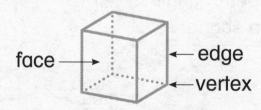

face → edge → vertex

Every cube has _6_ faces, _12_ edges, and _8_ vertices.

9. Cross out the shapes that are **NOT** cubes.

10. Draw a cube. Use the dots to help you.

Name _____

Set E _____

You can cover a rectangle with squares.

column

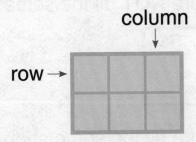

row →

Count by rows: $3 + 3 = 6$

Count by columns: $2 + 2 + 2 = 6$

6 squares cover the rectangle.

Use square tiles to cover the rectangle. Trace the tiles. Then count the squares.

11.

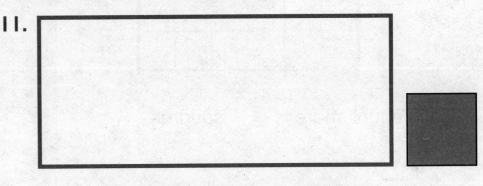

_____ squares cover the rectangle.

Set F _____

You can divide circles and rectangles into equal shares.

2 equal shares are **halves**.

3 equal shares are **thirds**.

4 equal shares are **fourths**.

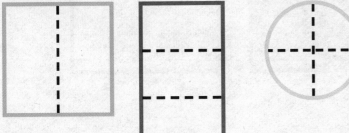

Divide each shape into the given number of equal shares. Show 2 ways.

12. halves ◯ ◯

13. thirds ▭ ▭

14. fourths ▢ ▢

Equal shares can be different shapes.

This is one way to divide this rectangle

into <u>3</u> equal shares.

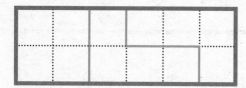

Each equal share is <u>4</u> squares.

Draw lines to show two more ways to divide the rectangle into 3 equal shares.

15. equal shares that are **NOT** all the same shape

16. equal shares that are all the same shape

Thinking Habits

Repeated Reasoning

Does something repeat in the problem?

How can the solution help me solve another problem?

Use the design shown. Create a different design with 3 equal shares.

17.

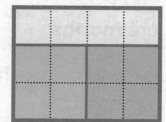 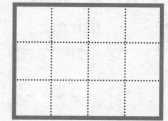

Name _____

1. Which polygons are pentagons?
Choose all that apply.

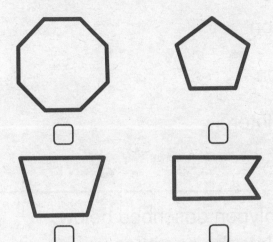

□   □

□   □

2. Rita draws a polygon. It has fewer than 8 sides and more angles than a square. Which shape did Rita draw?

Ⓐ   triangle

Ⓑ   rectangle

Ⓒ   hexagon

Ⓓ   quadrilateral

3. Which rectangles are divided into fourths?
Choose all that apply.

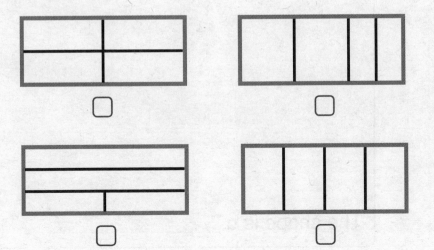

□   □

□   □

4. Draw a polygon with 4 angles. Make one angle a right angle. Then name the polygon.

Name: _____

5. Is the polygon a quadrilateral?
Choose Yes or No.

I have 3 sides and 3 angles. ○ Yes ○ No

I have 4 sides and 4 angles. ○ Yes ○ No

I am a square. ○ Yes ○ No

I am a rectangle. ○ Yes ○ No

6. Mandy draws a polygon with 6 sides and 6 angles. Which shape did she draw?

Ⓐ pentagon

Ⓑ hexagon

Ⓒ octagon

Ⓓ quadrilateral

7. Name the shape below. Write 3 things that describe the shape.

8. Draw the polygon described below. Then complete the sentence.

I have 2 fewer sides than a pentagon.
I have 1 less angle than a square.
I have one right angle.

The shape is a _____.

9. Complete the sentence to name and describe the solid figure below.

A _____ has ____ faces, ____ vertices, and ____ edges.

10. Divide the circle into 2 equal shares. Then complete the sentences.

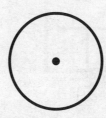

Each share is a _____ of the whole.
The whole is ____ halves.

11. Brad says there are only two ways to divide the same rectangle below into 3 equal shares. Do you agree? Use words and pictures to explain.

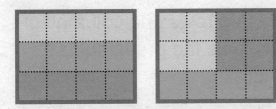

_____

_____

12. Count the number of squares in the rows and columns of the rectangle. Use the numbers on the cards to write the missing numbers in the equations.

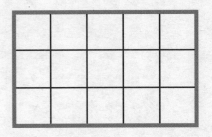

| 15 | 3 | 5 |

Rows: ____ + ____ + ____ = ____ squares

Columns: ____ + ____ + ____ + ____ + ____ = ____ squares

13. Kerry wants a design that shows thirds. Which designs could Kerry use? Choose all that apply.

☐   ☐   ☐   ☐

14. Is the solid figure a cube? Choose Yes or No.

☐ Yes ☐ No   ☐ Yes ☐ No   ☐ Yes ☐ No   ☐ Yes ☐ No

15. Use the dot paper. Draw a cube.

16. Divide the rectangle into rows and columns of squares the same size as the green square. Then count the squares.

_____ squares

Name _____

Happy Home

Tina and her family moved into a new home.
They bought different things for each room.

1. They hang pictures on the wall.
   Name the shape of each picture frame.

_____

_____

2. The rug in the kitchen has
   5 sides and 5 vertices.
   Draw the shape of the rug.

   Name the shape. _____

3. The wallpaper uses this pattern.

   Name the shape in the pattern.

   _____

   Write the number of sides, vertices, and
   angles in the shape.

   _____ sides   _____ vertices   _____ angles

4. The living room has 2 end tables.

Circle the table that is a cube. Explain.

_____

_____

_____

_____

5. Tina has a new quilt for her bed. Her quilt has this design.

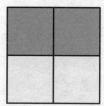

What share is green? _____

What share is yellow? _____

6. Tina's mother is making a quilt made of smaller squares. She wants the quilt to have 4 colors. Each color has an equal share.

Part A

Use 4 colors to make a possible quilt design below. Make the equal shares the same shape.

Design 1

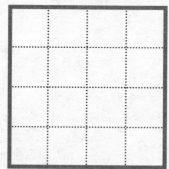

Part B

Use 4 colors to make a different quilt design below. Make the equal shares have different shapes.

Design 2

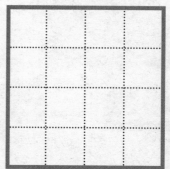

Here's a preview of next year. These lessons help you step up to Grade 3.

STEP UP to Grade 3

Lessons

Grade 3 lessons
look different.
Rotate the pages
so your name is at
the top.

Name _____

☆ ⭐ Solve & Share ☆

Ms. Witt bought 3 boxes of paint with 5 jars of paint in each box. What is the total number of jars Ms. Witt bought? *Solve this problem any way you choose.*

Solve

Lesson 1

Multiplication as Repeated Addition

I can ...
use addition or multiplication to join equal groups.

I can also make sense of problems.

Make sense of this problem. Think about what you know and what you need to find.

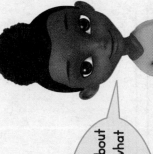

Look Back! **Model with Math** How can you use a picture to show the math you did in the problem?

How Can You Find the Total Number of Objects in Equal Groups?

A

Jessie used 3 bags to bring home the goldfish she won at the Fun Fair. She put the same number of goldfish in each bag. How many goldfish did she win?

I can use counters to show the groups.

8 goldfish in each bag

B

The counters show 3 groups of 8 goldfish.

You can use addition to join equal groups.

goldfish →
?

3 bags →

| 8 | 8 | 8 |

?

8 goldfish in each bag

$8 + 8 + 8 = 24$

C

Multiplication is an operation that gives the total number when you join equal groups.

goldfish →
?

3 bags →

| 8 | 8 | 8 |

?

8 goldfish in each bag

3 times 8 equals 24

$$3 \times 8 = 24$$

factor × factor = product

Factors are the numbers that are being multiplied. The product is the answer to a multiplication problem.

D

You can write equations.

Use a question mark for the unknown number that you find.

Addition equation:
$8 + 8 + 8 = ?$
$8 + 8 + 8 = 24$

Multiplication equation:
$3 \times 8 = ?$
$3 \times 8 = 24$

Jessie won 24 goldfish.

Convince Me! Model with Math Suppose Jessie won 5 bags of 8 goldfish. Draw a bar diagram and write an addition equation and a multiplication equation to represent the problem.

Name _____

 Tools

☆ Guided Practice ☆

Do You Understand?

1. Reasoning Can you write
$3 + 3 + 3 + 3 = 12$ as a multiplication equation? Explain.

2. Reasoning Can you write
$1 + 5 + 7 = 13$ as a multiplication equation? Explain.

3. Write an addition equation and a multiplication equation to solve this problem.
Matt buys 3 bags of apples. There are 6 apples in each bag. How many apples does Matt buy?

Do You Know How?

Complete **4** and **5**. Use the pictures to help.

4.

2 groups of _____

$3 + 3 =$ _____

$2 \times$ _____ $=$ _____

5.

_____ groups of 2

$2 +$ _____ $+$ _____ $=$ _____

$3 \times$ _____ $=$ _____

☆ Independent Practice ☆

Complete **6** and **7**. Use the pictures to help.

6.

2 groups of _____

$4 +$ _____ $=$ _____

$2 \times$ _____ $=$ _____

7.

3 groups of _____

$4 +$ _____ $+$ _____ $=$ _____

$3 \times$ _____ $=$ _____

In **8–11**, complete each equation. Use counters or draw a picture to help.

8. $5 + 5 + 5 + 5 = 4 \times$ _____

9. _____ $+$ _____ $= 2 \times 7$

10. $9 +$ _____ $= 2 \times$ _____

11. $6 + 6 + 6 + 6 =$ _____ $\times$ _____

Problem Solving ☆ ☆

12. Model with Math Lily has 8 eggs. Draw pictures to show two different ways Lily can make equal groups using 8 eggs.

13. Be Precise Erin reads 54 pages of her book. The book has 93 pages in all. How many pages does Erin have left to read? Show your work.

_____ pages

---

14. Critique Reasoning Chris says she can write two different equations to show 15 as repeated addition. Is Chris correct? Why or why not?

15. Higher Order Thinking George says you need equal groups to multiply. Is George correct? Why or why not?

 **Assessment**

16. Zoey has 10 stickers. She puts them in 2 groups of 5. How can you represent this? Choose all that apply.

☐ $5 + 2$

☐ $2 + 2 + 2 + 2 + 2$

☐ $5 + 5$

☐ 2×5

☐ $10 + 2 + 5$

17. Drew earns $6 each week. He wants to know how much money he will have saved after 5 weeks. How can you represent this? Choose all that apply.

☐ $\$6 + \$6 + \$6 + \$6 + \$6$

☐ $\$6 \times 6$

☐ $\$6 + \$5$

☐ $\$5 + \$5 + \$5 + \$5 + \$5$

☐ $\$6 \times 5$

Lesson 2
Arrays and Multiplication

I can ... use arrays to show and solve multiplication problems.

I can also use math tools correctly.

Name _____

Solve & Share

Mark put sports cards in an album. He put 4 rows of cards on each page. He put 3 cards in each row. How many cards are on each page? *Solve this problem any way you choose.*

Solve

You can use tools. Sometimes using objects can help you solve a problem. Show your work in the space below!

Look Back! **Make Sense and Persevere** Will your answer be the same if Mark puts 3 rows of 4 cards on each page? Explain.

Essential Question

How Does an Array Show Multiplication?

A

Dana keeps her swimming medal collection in a display on the wall.

The display has 4 rows. Each row has 5 medals. How many medals are in Dana's collection?

The medals are in an array. An array shows objects in equal rows and columns.

B

The counters show 4 rows and 5 columns.

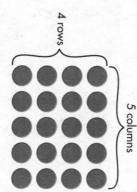

4 rows

5 columns

Each row is a group. You can use addition or skip counting to find the total.

Addition: $5 + 5 + 5 + 5 = 20$

Skip counting: 5, 10, 15, 20

C

Multiplication can also be used to find the total in an array.

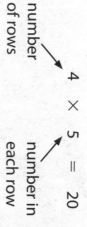

You say, "4 times 5 equals 20."

$$4 \times 5 = 20$$

number of rows → 4

number in each row → 5

There are 20 medals in Dana's collection.

Convince Me! Construct Arguments Jason also has a swimming medal collection. His display has 5 rows with 5 medals in each row. Who has more medals, Jason or Dana? Draw an array, then write an addition equation and a multiplication equation to show your work.

Name _____

Tools

⭐ Guided Practice ⭐

Do You Understand?

1. Look at page 926. What does the second factor tell you about the array?

2. Gina puts muffins in 4 rows with 8 muffins in each row. Draw an array to find the total number of muffins.

Do You Know How?

In **3** and **4**, write a multiplication equation for each array.

3.

4.

⭐ Independent Practice ⭐

In **5–7**, write a multiplication equation for each array.

5.

6.

7.

In **8** and **9**, draw an array to show each equation. Write the product.

8. $5 \times 9 =$ _____

9. $2 \times 8 =$ _____

Step Up | Lesson 2 **927**

Problem Solving ☆ ☆ ☆

10. Look for Relationships Lance draws these two arrays. How are the arrays alike? How are they different?

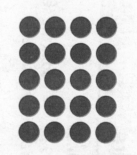

11. Construct Arguments How many more birch trees are there than pine trees? Explain how you know.

Trees in the Park	
Birch	ⅲ I
Oak	III
Maple	ⅲ
Pine	II

DATA

12. Higher Order Thinking Rachel has 19 pictures. Can she use all the pictures to make an array with exactly 4 equal rows? Why or why not?

13. Larry puts 7 nickels in each of his 3 empty piggy banks. How many nickels does Larry put in the banks? Write a multiplication equation to show how you solved the problem.

3 piggy banks →

7	7	7

? nickels

7 nickels in each bank

◀ Assessment

14. Mr. Williams planted 6 rows of apple trees on his farm. The apple trees are in 8 columns. How many trees are there in all?

- Ⓐ 6
- Ⓑ 8
- Ⓒ 14
- Ⓓ 48

15. Tina bought the stickers shown below. Which of the following shows how many stickers Tina bought?

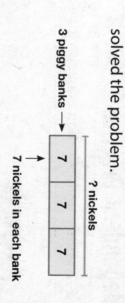

There are 5 rows. There are 2 stickers in each row.

- Ⓐ 5 + 2
- Ⓑ 5 × 2
- Ⓒ 5 × 5
- Ⓓ 5 − 2

Name _____

Solve & Share

Four friends picked 20 apples. They want to share them equally. How many apples should each person get? *Solve this problem any way you choose.*

Solve

Lesson 3
Division as Sharing

I can ...
use objects or pictures to show how objects can be divided into equal groups.

I can also model with math.

Model with math.
Drawing a picture that represents the problem can help you solve it.
Show your work!

Look Back! **Use Appropriate Tools** Can you use counters to help you solve this problem? Explain.

Essential Question

How Many Are in Each Group?

A

Three friends have 12 toys to share equally.
How many toys will each friend get?

Think of arranging 12 toys into 3 equal groups.

Division is an operation that is used to find how many equal groups there are or how many are in each group.

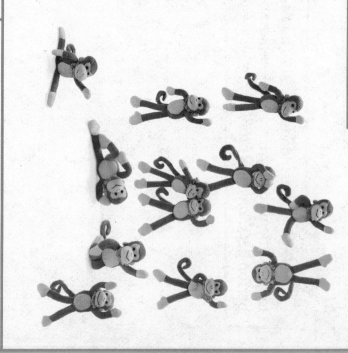

B

What You Think

Put one toy at a time in each group.

12 toys

4 toys for each friend

When all the toys are grouped, there will be 4 in each group.

C

What You Write

You can write a division equation to find the number in each group.

12 ÷ 3 = 4

Total → 12

Number of equal groups → 3

Number in each group → 4

Each friend will get 4 toys.

Convince Me! **Be Precise** What would happen if 3 friends wanted to share 13 toys equally?

Name _____

Tools

☆ Guided Practice ☆

Do You Understand?

1. 15 blocks are divided into 3 rows. How many blocks are in each row? Use the bar diagram to solve.

15

| ? | ? | ? |

15 ÷ 3 = _____ blocks

2. Be Precise Can 11 apples be shared equally among 4 children with no apples remaining? Explain.

Do You Know How?

In **3** and **4**, draw a picture to solve.

3. 16 bananas are shared equally by 4 monkeys. How many bananas does each monkey get?

4. 21 marbles are divided equally into 3 jars. How many marbles are in each jar?

☆ Independent Practice ☆

In **5** and **6**, draw a picture to solve.

5. 24 sandwiches are divided equally into 6 bags. How many sandwiches are in each bag?

6. 12 pencils are shared equally by 2 people. How many pencils does each person have?

In **7–10**, complete each equation.

7. 14 ÷ 2 = ▢

14

| ? | ? |

8. 24 ÷ 8 = ▢

24

| ? | ? | ? | ? | ? | ? | ? | ? |

9. 12 ÷ 4 = _____

10. 28 ÷ 7 = _____

Problem Solving ☆ ☆ ☆

11. **Critique Reasoning** Dean is putting 16 pens into equal groups. He says if he puts them into 2 equal groups he will have more pens in each group than if he puts them in 4 equal groups. Is Dean correct? Explain.

12. **Make Sense and Persevere** Ms. Baker's second grade class is divided into 4 teams. Each team has an equal number of students. Do you have enough information to find how many students are on each team? Explain.

13. Lily draws a rectangle. Sarah draws a pentagon. Who draws the shape with more sides? How many more sides does that shape have?

14. **Model with Math** The jazz band in a parade marches in 9 rows with 6 members in each row. Write an equation to show how many members there are.

15. **Number Sense** Joan equally shares 30 grapes with some friends. Is the number of grapes that each friend gets greater than 30 or less than 30? Explain.

16. **Higher Order Thinking** Lacie has 16 shells. She gives 6 shells to her mom. Then she and her sister share the other shells equally. How many shells does Lacie get? How many shells does her sister get? How do you know?

< **Assessment**

17. Darren has the 12 stickers shown at the right. He wants to put an equal number of stickers on each of 2 books. Draw circles in each box to represent the stickers Darren puts on each book.

Book 1

[   ]

Book 2

[   ]

Name _____

Solve & Share

Solve

Li made 12 tacos. He wants to give some of his friends 2 tacos each. If Li does not get any of the tacos, how many of his friends will get tacos? **Solve this problem any way you choose.**

Lesson 4

Division as Repeated Subtraction

I can ...
use repeated subtraction to understand and solve division problems.

I can also reason about math.

You can use reasoning. How can what you know about sharing help you solve the problem? Show your work in the space below!

Look Back! **Use Appropriate Tools** How can counters or other objects help you show your work?

How Can You Divide Using
Repeated Subtraction?

A

June has 10 strawberries to serve to her guests. If each guest eats 2 strawberries, how many guests can June serve?

10 strawberries →

2 strawberries for each guest

$\boxed{2}$

|← 10 →|
? guests

B

You can use repeated subtraction to find how many groups of 2 are in 10.

$10 - 2 = 8$
$8 - 2 = 6$
$6 - 2 = 4$
$4 - 2 = 2$
$2 - 2 = 0$

You can subtract 2 five times. There are five groups of 2 in 10.

There are no strawberries left.

June can serve 5 guests.

C

Write: $10 \div 2 = ?$
Read: Ten divided by 2 equals what number?
Solve: $10 \div 2 = 5$

June can serve 5 guests.

You can write a division equation to find the number of groups.

Convince Me! Model with Math In the example above, what if each guest eats 5 strawberries? Use the math you know to represent the problem and find how many guests June could serve.

934

Name _____

☆ Guided Practice

Do You Understand?

1. Show how you can use repeated subtraction to find how many groups of 5 there are in 25. Then write a division equation to solve the problem.

Do You Know How?

In **2** and **3**, use counters or draw a picture to solve.

2. The basketball team has 14 shoes. There are 2 shoes in each pair. How many pairs of shoes are there?

3. Maya has 18 cat toys. She gives each of her cats 6 toys. How many cats does Maya have?

☆ Independent Practice ☆

In **4** and **5**, complete the equations.

4. Tanya picks 18 pears. She places 9 pears in each bag. How many bags does Tanya have?

$18 - 9 =$ _____

____ $- 9 =$ _____

____ $\div 9 =$ _____

Tanya has ____ bags.

5. The workers on a farm have 7 keys each. There are 21 keys. How many workers are on the farm?

$21 - 7 =$ _____

____ $- 7 =$ _____

____ $-$ ____ $=$ _____

____ $\div$ ____ $=$ _____

There are ____ workers.

In **6** and **7**, use counters or draw a picture to solve.

6. Shawna bought 36 markers that came in packages of 4 markers each. How many packages did Shawna buy?

7. James has 16 pencils. He puts 2 pencils on each desk. How many desks are there?

8. **Generalize** The chart shows the number of pennies each of three friends has in her pocket. Each friend divides her money into piles of 4 coins. Write division equations to show how many equal piles each friend can make. Explain what repeats in the equations and how it helps you solve.

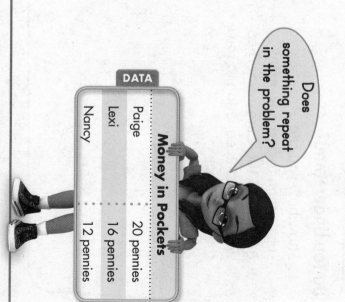

Does something repeat in the problem?

Money in Pockets

DATA	
Paige	20 pennies
Lexi	16 pennies
Nancy	12 pennies

9. If Lexi makes 8 columns of pennies, how many rows does she make? Write an equation to model and solve the problem.

10. **Model with Math** Tim has $45. He spends $21, then finds $28. How much money does Tim have now? Use math to represent the problem.

11. **Higher Order Thinking** A bakery plans to make 8 new muffins each year. How many years will it take for the store to make 40 new muffins? Write and solve an equation.

Assessment

12. Andy writes the following:

$$8 - 4 = 4$$
$$4 - 4 = 0$$

Which equation could Andy use to represent the same problem?

Ⓐ $4 \times 4 = 16$

Ⓑ $8 \div 8 = 1$

Ⓒ $8 \div 4 = 2$

Ⓓ $4 \div 2 = 2$

13. Rae writes the following:

$$27 - 9 = 18$$
$$18 - 9 = 9$$
$$9 - 9 = 0$$

Which problem is Rae trying to solve?

Ⓐ $27 \div 9$

Ⓑ $27 \div 3$

Ⓒ $27 - 9$

Ⓓ 27×3

Lesson 5
Add with Partial Sums

I can... add numbers using partial sums.

I can also reason about math.

Solve

Solve & Share

Find the sum of 327 + 241. Think about place value. **Solve this problem any way you choose.**

> You can use reasoning to make a plan. Part of your plan for solving this problem could be to show each of the numbers in expanded form. Show your work in the space below!

Look Back! **Reasoning** How can using place value help you solve this 3-digit addition problem?

How Can You Break Large Addition Problems into Smaller Ones?

A

Find the sum of 243 + 179. Each digit in the numbers can be modeled with place-value blocks.

You can use place value to add the numbers.

243

179

B

Step 1

Break 243 + 179 into smaller problems. Think about the place value of each number.

Hundreds	Tens	Ones
200	40	3
+ 100	+ 70	+ 9
300	110	12

C

Step 2

Then, add the sums of all the places.

```
  300
  110
+  12
  422
```

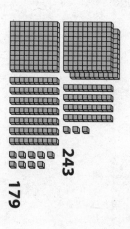

So, 243 + 179 = 422.

Convince Me! Construct Arguments Lexi says, "To solve 243 + 179, I can just count on with place-value blocks to find the answer: 100, 200, 300, another hundred from the 11 tens is 400, one more ten and 12 ones is 422!" How is Lexi's way like Steps 1 and 2 above?

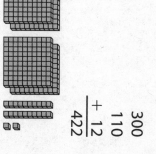

Name _____

☆ Guided Practice ☆

Do You Understand?

1. Reasoning Suppose you are adding 824 + 106. What would the tens problem be? Why?

2. Write the smaller problems you could use to find 512 + 362. What is the sum?

Do You Know How?

In **3**, use place value to find the sum.

3.

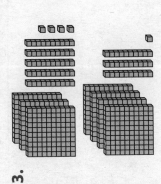

Find 354 + 431.

Hundreds	Tens	Ones	Total
300	50	4	
+400	+30	+1	

☆ Independent Practice ☆

In **4** through **11**, find each sum.

4.

348 + 131

Hundreds	Tens	Ones	Total
300	40	8	
+100	+30	+1	

5.

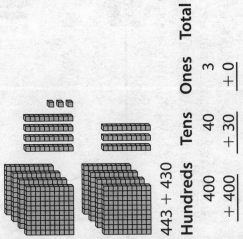

443 + 430

Hundreds	Tens	Ones	Total
400	40	3	
+400	+30	+0	

6. 264 + 524

7. 541 + 276

8. 249 + 180

9. 342 + 168

10. 191 + 502

11. 473 + 405

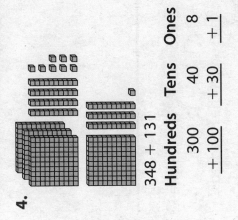

12. Critique Reasoning Henry believes the sum of 345 + 124 is 479. Is Henry correct? Explain.

345	124

?

13. Construct Arguments Explain how the solids shown in Group A and Group B could have been sorted.

Group A   Group B

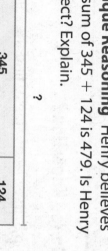

14. Model with Math Bill needs to find 325 + 133. Into what three smaller problems can Bill break this addition? What is the sum?

You can use place value to add.

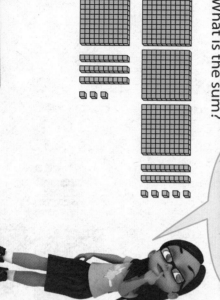

15. Higher Order Thinking A school cafeteria sells 215 lunches on Monday, 104 lunches on Tuesday, and 262 lunches on Wednesday. Did the cafeteria sell more lunches on Monday and Tuesday or on Tuesday and Wednesday? Explain.

Assessment

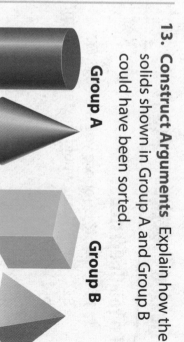

16. Jan read a book with 288 pages. Lara read a book with 416 pages. How many pages did Jan and Lara both read? Solve using partial sums.

Ⓐ 694
Ⓑ 704
Ⓒ 706
Ⓓ 716

17. Cody wants to add 482 + 315. He writes (400 + 300) + (80 + 10) + (2 + 5). Which shows the sum of the hundreds, tens, and ones?

Ⓐ 700 + 90 + 5
Ⓑ 700 + 90 + 7
Ⓒ 800 + 80 + 5
Ⓓ 800 + 60 + 7

Lesson 6

Models for Adding 3-Digit Numbers

I can ...
add 3-digit numbers using models, drawings, and place value.

I can also model with math.

Name _____

☆ Solve & Share ☆

Find the sum of 146 + 247.
Solve this problem any way you choose.

Model with math. You can use place-value blocks and draw pictures of the blocks to show how you found the sum. Show your work!

Look Back! **Generalize** When you add numbers, how do you know if you need to regroup?

How Can You Add 3-Digit Numbers with Place-Value Blocks?

A

Find 143 + 285.

You can add whole numbers by using place value to break them apart.

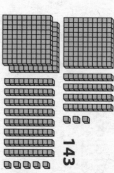

143

285

B

Add the ones, tens, and hundreds.

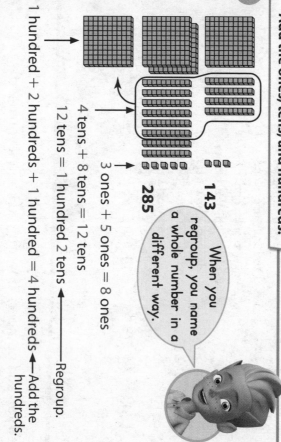

143

285

3 ones + 5 ones = 8 ones

4 tens + 8 tens = 12 tens

12 tens = 1 hundred 2 tens

1 hundred + 2 hundreds + 1 hundred = 4 hundreds

When you regroup, you name a whole number in a different way.

Regroup.

Add the hundreds.

C

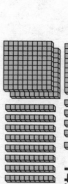

4 hundreds   2 tens   8 ones

428

143 + 285 = 428

Convince Me! Model with Math Mr. Wu drove 224 miles yesterday. He drove 175 miles today. Use place-value blocks or draw pictures of blocks to find how many miles Mr. Wu drove.

Tools

Another Example!

You may have to regroup twice when you add. Find 148 + 276.

Step 1

Add the ones.

8 ones + 6 ones = 14 ones

Regroup.

14 ones = 1 ten 4 ones

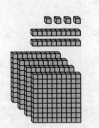

Step 2

Add the tens.

1 ten + 4 tens + 7 tens = 12 tens

Regroup.

12 tens = 1 hundred 2 tens

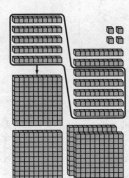

Step 3

Add the hundreds.

1 hundred + 1 hundred + 2 hundreds = 4 hundreds

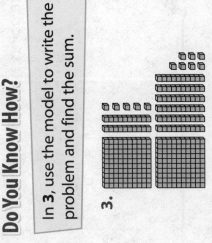

So, 148 + 276 = 424.

☆ Guided Practice ☆

Do You Understand?

1. **Generalize** How do you know when you need to regroup?

2. **Use Appropriate Tools** Use place-value blocks to find 136 + 279.

Do You Know How?

In **3**, use the model to write the problem and find the sum.

3.

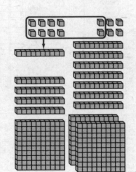

☆ Independent Practice ☆

In **4** through **6**, write the problem and find the sum.

4.

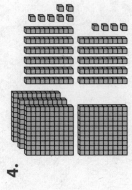

5.

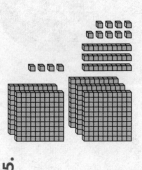

6.

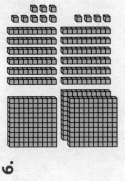

Problem Solving ☆ ☆ ☆

7. Model with Math Juan wants to use place-value blocks to show $148 + 256$. Draw a picture of the blocks Juan should use. What is the sum?

8. Use Appropriate Tools Manuel plays basketball and scores 15 points in game one, 8 points in game two, and 17 points in game three. How many points did Manuel score? Use the number line to solve the problem.

```
  ←─┼──┼──┼──┼──┼──┼──┼──┼──┼──┼──→
    0  10 20 30 40 50
```

9. Construct Arguments Al and Mark were playing a computer game. Al scored 265 points in the first round and 354 points in the second round. Mark scored 352 points in the first round and 237 points in the second round. Who scored more points and won the game? Explain.

10. Higher Order Thinking Paula is saving money to buy a new computer that costs $680. Last month she saved $415, and this month she saved $298. Does Paula have enough money saved to buy the computer? Use place-value blocks to help you solve the problem. Explain.

◀ **Assessment**

11. Write an equation that represents what the place-value blocks show.

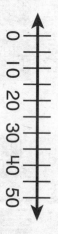

You may have to regroup when you find the sum.

12. Mrs. Samuels bought a $526 plane ticket in May and a $194 plane ticket in June. Use place-value blocks or draw pictures to find out how much Mrs. Samuels spent on both of the plane tickets.

Name _____

Solve & Share

Find the difference of 534 − 108. Think about place value. *Solve this problem any way you choose.*

Solve

You can use reasoning. How could you break this problem into smaller subtraction problems? Show your work in the space below!

Look Back! **Reasoning** How can using place value help you solve this subtraction problem?

Learn Glossary

How Can You Break Large Subtraction Problems into Smaller Ones?

A

At the end of the fourth round of a game of Digit Derby, Marco's score was 462 points. During the fifth round of the game, Marco loses points. What is Marco's score at the end of the fifth round?

Find 462 − 181.

End of Round 4
Marco has 462 points.

End of Round 5
Marco loses 181 points.

Place value can help you break a subtraction problem into smaller problems.

B

Step 1
Start with 462.

Subtract the **hundreds**.

$462 − 100 = 362$

So far, 100 has been subtracted.

C

Step 2
Next, start with 362.

Subtract the **tens**.

You need to subtract 8 tens, but there are not enough tens. So, subtract the 6 tens.

$362 − 60 = 302$

Then, subtract the 2 tens that are left.

$302 − 20 = 282$

So far, $100 + 60 + 20 = 180$ has been subtracted.

D

Step 3
That leaves just 1 to subtract.

Subtract the **ones**.

$282 − 1 = 281$

$100 + 60 + 20 + 1 = 181$ has been subtracted.

At the end of the fifth round, Marco's score is 281 points.

Convince Me! **Use Structure** Find $453 − 262$. Use place value to help break the problem into smaller problems. Show your work.

946

☆ Guided Practice

Do You Understand?

1. Construct Arguments Why do you need to record the numbers you subtract at each step?

2. Reasoning Carmella is trying to find 784 − 310. She decides to start by subtracting 10 from 784. Do you agree with Carmella? Explain.

Do You Know How?

In **3** and **4**, use place value to help break the problem into smaller problems.

3. Find 564 − 346.

564 − 300 = _____

264 − 40 = _____

224 − 4 = _____

220 − 2 = _____

4. Find 769 − 375.

769 − 300 = _____

469 − 60 = _____

409 − 10 = _____

399 − 5 = _____

☆ Independent Practice ☆

In **5** through **10**, follow the steps to find each difference. Show your work.

5. 728 − 413

First, subtract 400.

_____ − _____ = 328

Then, subtract 10.

_____ − _____ = _____

Then, subtract 3.

_____ − 3 = _____

6. 936 − 524

First, subtract 500.

936 − _____ = _____

Then, subtract 20.

_____ − 20 = _____

Then, subtract 4.

_____ − _____ = _____

7. 854 − 235

First, subtract 200.

_____ − 200 = _____

Then, subtract 30.

_____ − 30 = _____

Then, subtract 4.

_____ − 4 = _____

Then, subtract 1.

_____ − 1 = _____

8. 955 − 283

9. 946 − 507

10. 984 − 356

Tools

11. Use Appropriate Tools Write the time shown on the clock in 2 different ways.

_____

_____

12. Use Structure There are 96 boys and 83 girls in the school lunchroom. Near the end of lunch, 127 students leave. How many students are left in the lunchroom? Show how you can break part of the problem into smaller problems.

13. Model with Math Yuki had a necklace with 131 beads. The string broke, and she lost 43 beads. How many beads does Yuki have left?

131 beads

43	?

43 beads lost →   ? beads left →

14. Higher Order Thinking Which weighs more, two adult male Basset Hounds or one adult male Great Dane? Show the difference in pounds between the two Basset Hounds and the Great Dane. Draw bar diagrams to represent and help you solve the problem.

Great Dane   Basset Hound

145 pounds   66 pounds

Assessment

15. Karl's book has 416 pages. He read 50 pages last week. He read another 31 pages this week. How many more pages does Karl have left to read?

You can break the problem into smaller problems to solve.

Ⓐ 125   Ⓒ 335

Ⓑ 245   Ⓓ 345

948

Name _____

⭐ Solve & Share

Find the difference of 246 − 153.

Solve this problem any way you choose.

Model with math. Drawing pictures of place-value blocks is one way to represent this problem and help you solve it. Show your work!

Look Back! **Generalize** How can you check your answer for 246 − 153?

Solve

How Can You Subtract 3-Digit Numbers with Place-Value Blocks?

A

Fish caught near the Hawaiian Islands can be very large. How many more pounds does a broadbill swordfish weigh than a blue marlin?

Find 237 − 165.

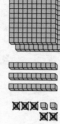

Use place value to subtract the ones first, the tens next, and then the hundreds.

Show 237 with place-value blocks.

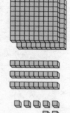

Wild Hawaiian Fish Weights	
Type of Fish	**Weight (in lb)**
Blue Marlin	165
Broadbill Swordfish	237

DATA

B

Subtract the ones.

7 ones > 5 ones, so no regrouping.

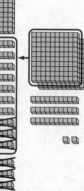

7 ones − 5 ones = 2 ones

```
  237
− 165
    2
```

C

Subtract the tens.

3 tens < 6 tens, so regroup.
1 hundred = 10 tens

13 tens − 6 tens = 7 tens

```
  1 13
  2 3̶ 7
− 1 6 5
    7 2
```

D

Subtract the hundreds.

1 hundred − 1 hundred = 0 hundreds

```
  1 13
  2 3̶ 7
− 1 6 5
      72
```

So, 237 − 165 = 72. A broadbill swordfish weighs 72 more pounds than a blue marlin.

Convince Me! **Model with Math** Anderson needs $231 to buy a new bike. He saved $144 from his summer job. How much more does Anderson need to save to buy the bike? Write a subtraction equation that models the problem. Use place-value blocks to help you solve the problem using the same steps shown above.

Tools

☆ Guided Practice ☆

Do You Understand?

1. Generalize In the example on page 950, for 237 − 165, why do you need to regroup 1 hundred into 10 tens?

2. Model with Math Gary saved $287 doing jobs in his neighborhood. He bought a computer printer for $183. How much money did Gary have left? Draw a picture of place-value blocks to help you subtract.

Do You Know How?

In **3** through **10**, use place-value blocks or draw pictures to subtract.

3.
```
  859
− 768
```

4.
```
  361
− 124
```

5.
```
  285
−  49
```

6.
```
  684
− 482
```

7. 384 − 358

8. 352 − 214

9. 512 − 101

10. 999 − 889

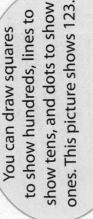

You can draw squares to show hundreds, lines to show tens, and dots to show ones. This picture shows 123.

☆ Independent Practice ☆

In **11** through **22**, use place-value blocks or draw pictures to subtract.

11.
```
  651
− 543
```

12.
```
  492
− 138
```

13.
```
  690
− 481
```

14.
```
  508
− 137
```

15.
```
  168
−  39
```

16.
```
  618
− 476
```

17.
```
  419
−  59
```

18.
```
  192
− 108
```

19.
```
  573
− 468
```

20.
```
  596
− 128
```

21.
```
  819
− 124
```

22.
```
  438
− 283
```

Problem Solving ☆☆☆

For **23** and **24**, use the table at the right.

Think
What do I know?
What do I need to find?

Trip Distances

Trip	Miles
Cleveland to Chicago	346
Cincinnati to Cleveland	249
Washington, D.C., to Cleveland	372

DATA

23. How many more miles is it from Cleveland to Chicago than from Cincinnati to Cleveland?

24. **Make Sense and Persevere** Mr. Sousa is driving from Washington, D.C., to Cleveland and then to Cincinnati. He has traveled 182 miles. How many miles are left in his trip?

25. **Make Sense and Persevere** Which girl got more votes? How many more votes did that girl get?

Student Council President Votes

	7th Grade Votes	8th Grade Votes
Claudia	183	157
Jasmine	162	156

DATA

26. Kendra got $20 for her birthday. She earned $62 babysitting. Then she earned $148 shoveling snow. How much money does Kendra have?

$20	$62	$148
	?	

27. **Higher Order Thinking** Kim needs to find $437 - 258$. Will she need to regroup to find the answer? If so, explain how she will need to regroup. What will Kim's answer be?

Assessment

28. It is 239 miles from Dallas to Houston and 275 miles from Dallas to San Antonio. How many fewer miles is it from Dallas to Houston than from Dallas to San Antonio?

Ⓐ 34 fewer miles

Ⓑ 36 fewer miles

Ⓒ 44 fewer miles

Ⓓ 45 fewer miles

29. An amusement park ride can hold 120 people. There are already 104 people on the ride. Which equation shows how many more people the ride can hold?

Ⓐ $120 - 104 = 16$

Ⓑ $120 - 100 = 20$

Ⓒ $120 - 94 = 26$

Ⓓ $120 + 104 = 224$

952

Lesson 9

Divide Regions into Equal Parts

I can ... read and write a unit fraction.

I can also be precise in my work.

⊙ Solve

Name _____

☆ **Solve & Share** ☆

Show two different ways to divide a 2 × 6 region into 6 equal parts. Color the 6 parts of each region a different color. How do you know the parts are equal?

Be precise. Think about each part as you divide the regions.

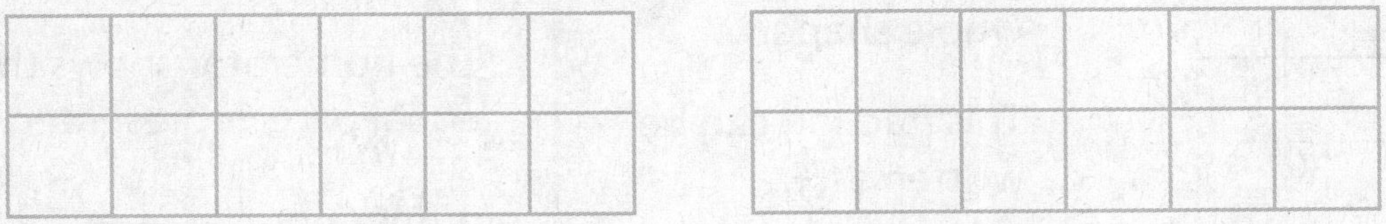

Look Back! Use Structure How are the parts of the regions alike? How are they different?

Digital Resources at SavvasRealize.com

Learn Glossary A-Z

How Can You Name the Equal Parts of a Whole?

A

Divide a whole into halves. What fraction can you write to represent one half of a whole?

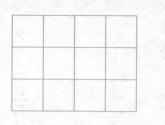

A fraction is an equal part of a whole.

B

one half

one half

Each part is made up of 6 unit squares. Both parts have equal areas.

C

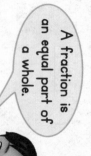

$\frac{1}{2}$

$\frac{1}{2}$

Each part is **one half** of the area of the whole shape.

This fraction can be written as $\frac{1}{2}$.

$\frac{1}{2}$ is a unit fraction.

A unit fraction represents one of the equal parts.

D

The number above the bar in a fraction is called the numerator.

The numerator shows the number of equal parts represented by that fraction.

numerator

denominator

$\frac{1}{2}$

The number below the bar in a fraction is called the denominator.

The denominator shows the total number of equal parts in that whole.

Convince Me! Be Precise Divide the grid at the right into thirds. Label each third using a unit fraction. Explain how you knew which fraction to write.

954

Essential Question

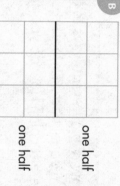

Name _____

☆ Guided Practice

Do You Understand?

1. In the examples on page 954, explain how you know the two parts are equal.

In **2** and **3**, tell if each shows equal or unequal parts. If the parts are equal, label one of the parts using a unit fraction.

2.

3.

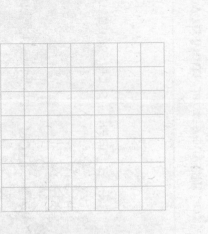

Do You Know How?

4. Draw a rectangle that is divided into fourths. Then, write the fraction that represents one equal part.

☆ Independent Practice ☆

In **5–7**, tell if each shows equal or unequal parts. If the parts are equal, name them.

5.

6.

7.

In **8** and **9**, draw lines to divide the shape into the given number of equal parts. Then write the fraction that represents one equal part.

8. 3 equal parts

9. 8 equal parts

Problem Solving ☆☆☆

In **10-13**, use the table of flags.

10. Which nation's flag is $\frac{1}{3}$ white?

11. **Be Precise** What fraction represents the red part of Poland's flag?

12. Which nation's flag does **NOT** have equal parts?

13. Which nation's flag is $\frac{1}{4}$ green?

Flags of Different Nations

Nation	Flag
Mauritius	
Nigeria	
Poland	
Seychelles	

14. **Model with Math** James buys 18 bottles of water. The water comes in packs of 6 bottles. How many packs did he buy? Write an addition equation and a multiplication equation to show your answer.

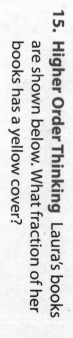 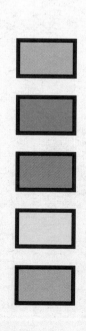

15. **Higher Order Thinking** Laura's books are shown below. What fraction of her books has a yellow cover?

< **Assessment**

16. On the grid below, draw a rectangle. Divide your rectangle into fourths. Explain how you checked the reasonableness of your work.

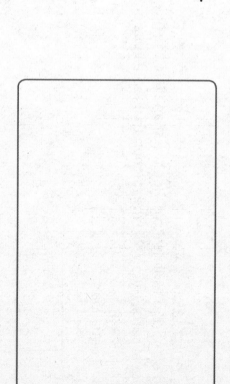

Name _____

Lesson 10

Fractions and Regions

I can ... show and name part of a region.

I can also make sense of problems.

Solve

Solve & Share

Pat made a garden in the shape of a rectangle and divided it into 4 same-size parts. She planted flowers in one of the parts. Draw a picture of what Pat's garden might look like.

You can make sense of the given information to plan your drawing of Pat's garden.

Look Back! **Construct Arguments** How many parts of Pat's garden do **NOT** have flowers? Explain.

How Can You Show and Name Part of a Region?

Essential Question

A

Mr. Peters served part of a pan of enchilada casserole to a friend. What does each part of the whole pan of casserole represent? What part was served? What part is left?

A fraction is a symbol that names equal parts of a whole. A unit fraction represents one part of a whole that has been divided into equal parts. A unit fraction always has a numerator of 1.

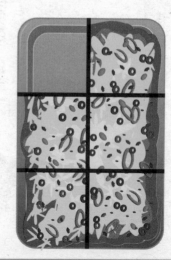

B

What You Think

There are 6 equal pieces in the whole, so each piece is $\frac{1}{6}$.

There is 1 piece missing, so one $\frac{1}{6}$-piece was served.

There are 5 pieces left, so five $\frac{1}{6}$-pieces are left.

The numerator shows how many equal parts are described. The denominator shows the total number of equal parts in a whole.

C

What You Write

$\frac{1}{6}$ ← numerator
← denominator

$\frac{1}{6}$ of the pan of enchilada casserole was served.

$\frac{5}{6}$ of the pan of enchilada casserole is left.

Do You Understand?

Convince Me! **Model with Math** Below is a picture of a pie pan. Draw lines and use shading to show that five $\frac{1}{8}$-pieces are still in the pan, and that three $\frac{1}{8}$-pieces were eaten. Remember to draw same-size parts.

Name _____

☆ Guided Practice ☆

Do You Understand?

1. In the problem at the top of page 958, what fraction names all of the pieces in the casserole?

2. Model with Math Mrs. Rao made a cake. What fraction of the whole cake does each piece represent?

3. In the picture in Item 2, how many $\frac{1}{8}$-pieces were eaten? What fraction of the whole cake was eaten?

Do You Know How?

In **4** through **7**, use the figure below.

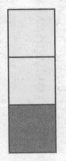

4. Write the unit fraction that represents each part of the whole.

5. How many $\frac{1}{3}$-parts are yellow?

6. What fraction of the whole is yellow?

7. What fraction names *all* of the parts in the whole?

☆ **Independent Practice** ☆

In **8** through **11**, write the unit fraction that represents each part of the whole. Then write the number of blue parts and the fraction of the whole that is blue.

8.

9.

10.

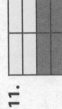

11.

12. Draw a rectangle that shows 6 equal parts. Then shade $\frac{3}{6}$ of the rectangle. Explain how you know you shaded $\frac{3}{6}$ of the rectangle.

Problem Solving ☆ ☆

13. Reasoning What is the distance around the baseball card? Write an equation to show and solve the problem.

6 cm

8 cm

14. Model with Math Janice has 2 scarves. Carla has 3 times as many scarves as Janice. How many scarves does Carla have? Use the bar diagram to write and solve an equation.

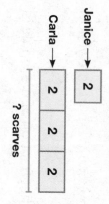

Janice → | 2 |

Carla → | 2 | 2 | 2 |

? scarves

15. Higher Order Thinking Draw a circle that shows 6 equal parts. Shade more than $\frac{3}{6}$ of the circle, but less than $\frac{5}{6}$ of the circle. What fraction have you modeled?

◀ **Assessment**

In **16** and **17**, use the chart to the right.

16. Kiko and some friends bought a medium party tray. They ate 5 sections of the tray. Which of the following shows the unit fraction, and the fraction of the tray that was **NOT** eaten?

Ⓐ $\frac{1}{8}$, $\frac{3}{8}$

Ⓑ $\frac{1}{6}$, $\frac{4}{6}$

Ⓒ $\frac{8}{8}$, $\frac{2}{8}$

Ⓓ $\frac{1}{6}$, $\frac{1}{6}$

17. Jesse and his friends ordered a large party tray. Which unit fraction does each section of the tray represent?

Ⓐ $\frac{1}{4}$

Ⓑ $\frac{1}{6}$

Ⓒ $\frac{1}{8}$

Ⓓ $\frac{1}{10}$

Size of Tray	Price
Small	$8
Medium	$10
Large	$12

In a unit fraction the numerator is always 1.

Glossary

A

add

When you add, you join groups together.

$$3 + 4 = 7$$

addend

numbers that are added

$$2 + 5 = 7$$

addends

after

424 comes after 423.

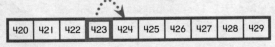

| 420 | 421 | 422 | 423 | 424 | 425 | 426 | 427 | 428 | 429 |

a.m.

clock time from midnight until noon

7:10 PM

angle

the corner shape formed by two sides that meet

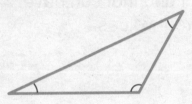

array

a group of objects set in equal rows and columns that forms a rectangle

B

bar diagram

a model for addition and subtraction that shows the parts and the whole

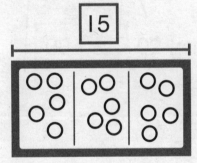

15

bar graph

A bar graph uses bars to show data.

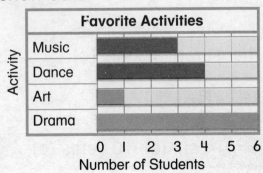

Favorite Activities

Activity: Music, Dance, Art, Drama

0 1 2 3 4 5 6
Number of Students

before

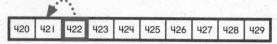

421 comes before 422.

break apart

You can break apart a number into its place value parts.

$$27 + 35 = ?$$

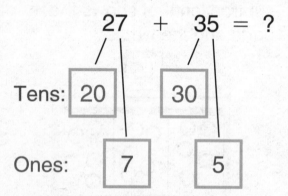

Tens: 20   30

Ones: 7   5

cents

The value of a coin is measured in cents (¢).

1 cent (¢)   10 cents (¢)

centimeter (cm)

a metric unit of length that is part of 1 meter

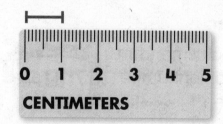

CENTIMETERS

coins

money that is made out of metal and that can have different values

1¢   5¢   10¢   25¢   50¢

column

objects in an array or data in a table that are shown up and down

← column

1	2	3	4	5
11	12	13	14	15
21	22	23	24	25
31	32	33	34	35

compare

When you compare numbers, you find out if a number is greater than, less than, or equal to another number.

$$147 > 143$$

147 is greater than 143.

compatible numbers

numbers that are easy to add or subtract using mental math

$$8 + 2$$
$$20 + 7$$
$$53 + 10$$

compensation

a mental math strategy you can use to add or subtract

$$38 + 24 = ?$$
$$+2 \quad -2$$

You add 2 to 38 to make 40. Then subtract 2 from 24 to get 22. 40 + 22 = 62. So, 38 + 24 = 62.

cone

a solid figure with a circle shaped base and a curved surface that meets at a point

cube

a solid figure with six faces that are matching squares

cylinder

a solid figure with two matching circle shaped bases

data

information you collect and can be shown in a table or graph

Favorite Fruit	
Apple	7
Peach	4
Orange	5

decrease

to become lesser in value

$$600 \longrightarrow 550$$

600 decreased by 50 is 550.

denominator

the number below the fraction bar in a fraction, which shows the total number of equal parts

$$\frac{3}{4} \longleftarrow \text{denominator}$$

difference

the answer in a subtraction equation or problem

$$14 - 6 = 8$$
$$\uparrow$$
difference

digits

Numbers are made up of 1 or more digits. 43 has 2 digits.

dime

10 cents or 10¢

division

an operation that tells how many equal groups there are or how many are in each group

$$12 \div 3 = 4$$

divided by

what you say to read a division symbol

$$18 \div 3 = 6$$

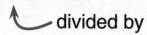 divided by

dollar

One dollar equals 100¢.

dollar bills

paper money that can have different dollar values, such as $1, $5, $10, or $20

dollar sign

a symbol used to show that a number represents money

$37

↑
dollar sign

doubles

addition facts that have two addends that are the same

$$4 + 4 = 8$$

↑   ↑
addend addend

E

edge

a line formed where two faces of a solid figure meet

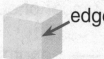 edge

eighths

When a whole is separated into 8 equal shares, the parts are called eighths.

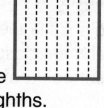

equal groups

groups that have the same number of items or objects

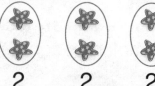

2   2   2

equal shares

parts of a whole that are the same size

All 4 shares are equal.

equals (=)

has the same value

$$36 = 36$$

36 is equal to 36.

equation

a math sentence that uses an equal sign (=) to show that the value on the left is equal to the value on the right

$$3 + ? = 7$$

$$14 - 6 = 8$$

estimate

When you estimate, you make a good guess.

This table is about 3 feet long.

even

a number that can be shown as a pair of cubes.

8 is even.

expanded form

a way of writing a number that shows the place value of each digit

$$400 + 60 + 3 = 463$$

face

a flat surface of a solid figure that does not roll

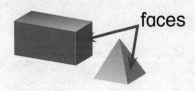

faces

fact family

a group of related addition and subtraction facts

$$2 + 4 = 6$$

$$4 + 2 = 6$$

$$6 - 2 = 4$$

$$6 - 4 = 2$$

factors

numbers that are multiplied together to give a product

$$7 \times 3 = 21$$

factors

flat surface

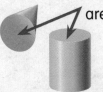

flat surfaces that are **NOT** faces

foot (ft)

a standard unit of length equal to 12 inches

fourths

When a whole is divided into 4 equal shares, the shares are called fourths.

fraction

a number, such as $\frac{1}{2}$ or $\frac{3}{4}$, that names part of a whole or part of a set

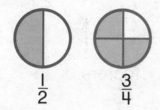

$\frac{1}{2}$ $\frac{3}{4}$

greater than (>)

has greater value

$$5 > 1$$

5 is greater than 1.

greatest

the number in a group with the largest value

35 47 58 61

greatest

greatest value

The coin that has the greatest value is the coin that is worth the most.

The quarter has the greatest value.

half-dollar

50 cents or 50¢

half past

30 minutes past the hour

It is half past 9.

halves (half)

When a whole is divided into 2 equal shares, the shares are called halves.

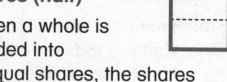

height

how tall an object is from bottom to top

heptagon

a polygon that has 7 sides

hexagon

a polygon that has 6 sides

hour

An hour is 60 minutes.

hundred

10 tens make 1 hundred.

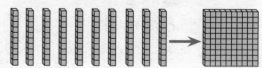

G6

Glossary

inch (in.)

a standard unit of length that is part of 1 foot

increase

to become greater in value

550 ⟶ 600

550 increased by 50 is 600.

least

the number in a group with the smallest value

35 47 58 61
↖ least

least value

The coin that has the least value is the coin that is worth the least.

The dime has the least value.

length

the distance from one end to the other end of an object

less than (<)

has less value

2 < 6

2 is less than 6.

line plot

A line plot uses dots above a number line to show data.

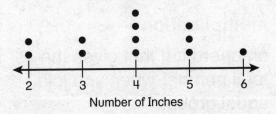

Lengths of Shells

Number of Inches

Start at 23. Count on 2 tens. 33, 43

mental math

math you do in your head

23 + 20 = 43

meter (m)

a metric unit of length equal to 100 centimeters

A long step is about a meter.

minute

a standard length of time

There are 60 minutes in 1 hour.

multiplication

an operation that gives the total number when you join equal groups

$$3 \times 2 = 6$$

To multiply 3×2 means to add 2 three times.

$$2 + 2 + 2 = 6$$

near doubles

addition facts that have two addends that are close

$$4 + 5 = 9$$

↑   ↑
addend addend

nearest centimeter

The whole number centimeter mark closest to the measure is the nearest centimeter.

about 2 cm long

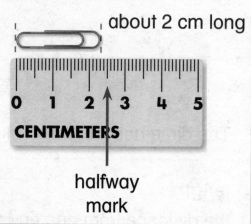

halfway mark

nearest inch

The whole number inch mark closest to the measure is the nearest inch.

about 2 inches long

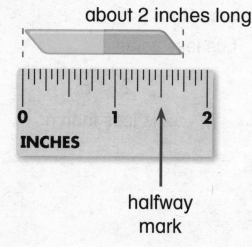

halfway mark

next ten

the first ten greater than a number

30 is the next ten after 27.

nickel

5 cents or 5¢

nonagon

a polygon that has 9 sides

number line

a line that shows numbers in order from left to right

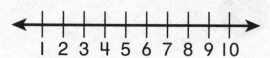

1 2 3 4 5 6 7 8 9 10

numerator

the number above the fraction bar in a fraction, which shows how many equal parts are described

$\dfrac{3}{4}$ ←———— numerator

octagon

a polygon that has 8 sides

odd

a number that can **NOT** be shown as pairs of cubes

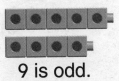

9 is odd.

ones

digits that shows how many ones are in a number

54 + 14 = 68
↑   ↑   ↑

open number line

An open number line is a tool that can help you add or subtract. It can begin at any number.

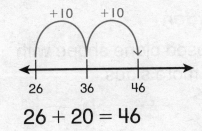

26 + 20 = 46

order

to place numbers from least to greatest or from greatest to least

27 72 107 117 171

least ↰   greatest ↰

parallelogram

a quadrilateral that has 4 sides and opposite sides parallel

part

a piece of a whole or of a number

2 and 3 are parts of 5.

partial sum

When you add numbers, the sum of one of the place values is called a partial sum.

Tens	Ones	
5	7	
+ 2	8	
7	0	← partial sum
+ 1	5	← partial sum
8	5	← sum

penny

1 cent or 1¢

pentagon

a polygon that has 5 sides

picture graph

a graph that uses pictures to show data

Favorite Ball Games	
Baseball	♀♀
Soccer	♀♀♀♀♀♀
Tennis	♀♀♀♀

Each ♀ = 1 student

place-value chart

a chart matches each digit of a number with its place

Hundreds	Tens	Ones
3	4	8

plane shape

a flat shape

circle   rectangle   square   triangle

p.m.

clock time from noon until midnight

polygon

a closed plane shape with 3 or more sides

product

the answer to a multiplication problem

$$4 \times 2 = 8$$

↑
product

pyramid

a solid figure with a base that is a polygon and faces that are triangles that meet in a point

Q

quadrilateral

a polygon that has 4 sides

quarter

25 cents or 25¢

quarter past

15 minutes after the hour

It is quarter past 4.

quarter to

15 minutes before the hour

It is quarter to 4.

R

rectangular prism

a solid figure with bases and faces that are rectangles

regroup

to name a number or part in a different way

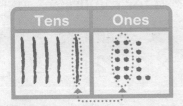

10 ones can be regrouped as 1 ten. 1 ten can be regrouped as 10 ones.

related

Addition facts and subtraction facts are related if they have the same numbers.

$$2 + 3 = 5$$
$$5 - 2 = 3$$

repeated addition

adding the same number repeatedly

$$3 + 3 + 3 + 3 = 12$$

right angle

an angle that forms a square corner

row

objects in an array or data in a table that are shown across

1	2	3	4	5
11	12	13	14	15
21	22	23	24	25
31	32	33	34	35

← row

 S

separate

to subtract or to take apart into two or more parts

$$5 - 2 = 3$$

side

a line segment that makes one part of a plane shape

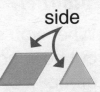

side

solid figure

a shape that has length, width, and height

These are all solid figures.

sphere

a solid figure that looks like a ball

standard form

a way to write a number using only digits

436

subtract

When you subtract, you find out how many are left or which group has more.

$$5 - 3 = 2$$

sum

the answer to an addition equation or problem

$$3 + 4 = 7$$

$$\begin{array}{r} 4 \\ +\ 3 \\ \hline 7 \end{array}$$

sum →

symbol

a picture or character that stands for something

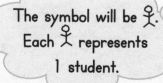

The symbol will be 🯅.
Each 🯅 represents
1 student.

tally mark

a symbol used to keep track of each piece of information in an organized list

Ways to Show 30¢			
Quarter	Dime	Nickel	Total
I		I	30¢
	III		30¢
	II	II	30¢
	I	IIII	30¢
		卌 I	30¢

tens

the digit that shows how many groups of ten are in a number

238

thirds

When a whole is divided into 3 equal shares, the shares are called thirds.

thousand

10 hundreds make 1 thousand.

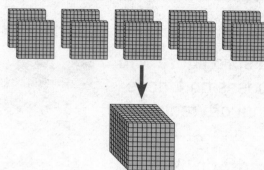

times

another word for multiply

times

$$7 \times 3 = 21$$

trapezoid

a polygon with 4 sides and one pair of sides are parallel

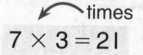

triangular prism

a solid figure that has two triangle shaped bases and three faces that have rectangle shapes.

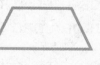

unequal

Unequal parts are parts that are not equal.

5 unequal parts

unit

You can use different units to measure.

about 12 inches
about 1 foot

unit fraction

a fraction that reperesents one equal part of a whole or a set

$\frac{1}{2}$ $\frac{1}{4}$ $\frac{1}{8}$

unknown

a symbol that stands for a number in an equation

$$34 + ? = 67$$

↑

unknown

vertices (vertex)

corner points where 2 sides of a polygon meet or where edges of a solid figure meet

vertex

whole

a single unit that can be divided into parts

The two halves make one whole circle.

width

the distance across an object

word form

a way to write a number using only words

The word form for 23 is twenty-three.

yard (yd)

a standard unit of length equal to 3 feet

A baseball bat is about a yard long.

Photographs

Photo locators denoted as follows: Top (T), Center (C), Bottom (B), Left (L), Right (R), Background (Bkgd)

001BL Lori Martin/Shutterstock;**001BR** An Nguyen/ Shutterstock;**001C** Africa Studio/Fotolia;**001L** Africa Studio/ Fotolia;**001R** karandaev/Fotolia;**077BL** michaklootwijk/ Fotolia;**077BR** Jitka Volfova/Shutterstock;**077L** Charles Brutlag/ Shutterstock;**077R** Erni/Fotolia;**119L** FiCo74/Fotolia;**119R** Antonio Scarpi/Fotolia;**189** Beboy/Shutterstock;**253** Deborah Benbrook/Fotolia;**321** GlebStock/Shutterstock;**389** Paylessimages/Fotolia;**435** Ambient Ideas/Shutterstock;**503** Es0lex/Fotolia;**583** kalafoto/Fotolia;**635** Klagyivik Viktor/ Shutterstock;**675** Nagel Photography/Shutterstock;**678** Optionm/Shutterstock;**687** Ant Clausen/Fotolia;**759** Bonita R. Cheshier/Shutterstock;**788** Lledó/Fotolia;**790** Ivan Kruk/ Fotolia;**799L** Karichs/Fotolia;**799R** Ivonne Wierink/Fotolia;**851** Yurakr/Shutterstock;**868** StudioSmart/Shutterstock;**G10R** United State Mint.